作家

Born in Suffolk, Sue Wall began her working life as a journalist on local newspapers, before studying law and then moving into lecturing. Although she only left England once during her twenties (a day trip to Calais), she has always been keen to travel, and by combining English language and law teaching, was able to work in many European countries, and then further afield. The opportunity of living in Beijing for two years was too good to miss, which led to these letters home, describing her daily life in a very different culture.

LETTERS FROM CHINA

LETTERS FROM CHINA

Sue Wall

ATHENA PRESS
LONDON

First Published 2005 by
ATHENA PRESS
Queen's House, 2 Holly Road
Twickenham TW1 4EG
United Kingdom

Printed for Athena Press

To my daughter Ros

My first trip to China – 1999

一
九
九
九

Dear Everyone,

Forgive me for writing a general letter, but I know I won't have time to do separate letters, so I may as well admit this is for all my friends, rather than pretend to personalise the opening.

To make it easier to follow, this was my itinerary:

  16 April, Heathrow to Beijing;
  17 to 21 April, Beijing;
  21 April, overnight by train to Wuhan (south of Beijing);
  22/23 April, Wuhan;
  23 April, by air to Chengdu (west of Beijing);
  23 to 27 April, Chengdu;
  27 April, by air to Qingdao (on east coast, north of Shanghai);
  29 April, by air to Shanghai;
  1 May, by air to Beijing;
  4 May, back to the UK.

23 April

I'm starting this while waiting to fly to Chengdu (in Sichuan province) from Wuhan – in Hubei province. This is the first real patch of time I have had to myself since I arrived. Any time in the evening at my hotel I've fallen into bed (not always to go to sleep immediately because it has been too exciting). It's odd though to have about three hours alone with no one talking to me in broken English. Everyone so far has been incredibly hospitable, and friendly (apparently this is Chinese culture) – but at times I just want to be alone.

Well, I had been warned that Chinese flights leave early, and that one did – half an hour! I caught it, even though it also left from a different gate, but it did interrupt my letter-writing.

So now I am carrying on while in my suite at Chengdu – actually at the university. The suite is in the university hotel, and definitely is a suite – huge sitting room and huge bedroom, each with a balcony; fruit and fresh flowers supplied every day, and a flask of hot water so I can make tea whenever I want. Of course I'd quite like a cup of coffee – almost unheard of here. I had some on the plane, but none since then, nor likely to until I next fly.

Similarly, neither sight nor sound of knives and forks, so I am, of necessity, a dab hand with chopsticks (provided I get the cheap wooden ones rather than fancy modern plastic, which are too slick and shiny). Not that it seems to matter much – Chinese eating seems to be a lot of slurping and sucking, and whooshing of food from bowl into mouth via chopsticks. Effective even if not elegant. And the great thing seems to be to do it often, in large quantities.

My average day has begun with breakfast around 7.30–8 (in Beijing, in a standard hotel, it was serve-yourself buffet, plus coffee, but cost 112 yuan which is very expensive by Chinese prices; dinner for two this evening cost 30 yuan in the university hotel, and we had to leave half of it there was so much)... followed by non-stop tea (if you take a mouthful your mug is almost instantly refilled with hot water), then lunch at around 11.30 a.m., often described as simple but in fact extremely lavish as I am a guest. Bowls and bowls of different dishes, and I am expected to try them all: soup, steamed dumplings, on and on, and then finally some fresh fruit... or, as I have discovered in Eastern China, Qingdao and Shanghai, a final course of starch (i.e. rice or dumplings), and dinner follows at about 5.30/6 p.m. – and this is inevitably more lavish than lunch.

Oh, yes – and if it is a Chinese breakfast, which it has been every day since Wednesday (and will be for the foreseeable future) then it always includes rice porridge, which I think is just boiled rice in water, maybe milky water. Anyway, designed to fill you up for the rest of the day, even if you had nothing else.

So, where have I been since I arrived here well over a week ago? Arrival was into Beijing, early on Saturday 17 (well, 9.30 a.m. – early enough). Fortunately the flight was a third full, so I was able to sleep… just as well. I was met at the airport, taken to the hotel, and then it was almost immediately off sightseeing… but, of course, lunch was first – Beijing duck. Loads of it – my first of almost daily Beijing duck until I came to Sichuan. And on every occasion I was expected to praise it and eat loads. Then off to the Forbidden City, past Tiananmen Square, and other sights like huge posters of Mao. Everything is being prepared for the fiftieth anniversary celebrations in October, so much is under scaffolding.

On Sunday it was an early start and off to the Great Wall – overwhelming, exhausting, hot – and the added excitement of the car breaking down on the way there, so our host put us in a taxi. Our host on this occasion is an insurance agent in Beijing, with fingers in a thousand pies, who is hoping to get in on education. I don't think we will use him, but not because of the car incident.

On the way back from the Great Wall we went to the Ming Tombs; more amazingly huge buildings, although very little to actually see. Even going down into the one which has been excavated only gave us sight of the outside of the container of the coffin, some vases and one or two relics which could not really be seen due to the poor lighting.

A feature of all this sightseeing, which has been repeated everywhere, is that I am not allowed to pay for anything: not the ticket (and there are tickets at every stage you go through – one to get in, one to visit this hall, one for that), not the meal, not the ice cream. It is embarrassing and I almost hate to indicate I like something in case it is bought for me. This is Chinese hospitality, and my only consolation is that my hosts will claim it back, and of course they get the outing too.

Both evenings of the first weekend were spent in Chinese homes; a friend/contact (English name, 'Jean') who now lives in England took us first to her parents' (where her mother, a retired Chinese government worker, gave me a beautiful painting of a

May blossom she has done herself, complete with calligraphy, as part of her retirement art class). The food was extremely good, and the flat was interesting. In an old dirty-looking block, it turned out to be very well furnished and clean inside the actual flat (the corridors were horrendous); they have a maid – the daughter of distant relatives in the country, who is one of a series who come to work in Beijing, get some education while working as a maid, then get other work, and eventually marry. Meanwhile another girl will come from the country.

The family are clearly quite well off and well connected; the father was deputy chief officer in a regional government office (maybe even the equivalent of deputy mayor) but suffered under the Cultural Revolution when he was beaten up severely, and the family were sent to different parts of China. Somehow Jean, our contact, got to university, and studied herbal medicine which she now practises in England; another sister is a doctor, as is one brother; but the other two had their education so interrupted they have not got degrees. The father was allowed back from 'banishment', and got his old job back by the late sixties, hence the relative comfort now (at least that is what I understood. I did not want to ask too much).

On Sunday night we had dinner with Jean's sister and niece – the non-graduate who is now manager of a supermarket. The flat again was lovely inside although small – two bedrooms, a small living room, kitchen and bathroom. But reasonably furnished, big telly, video… but the crockery was shabby, and I guess they have few clothes. The outside of the flats were awful – dirty, smelly, quite frightening and dark – worse than any I can picture in London, and one of about ten very high blocks with little outside lighting. When we left it was a matter of feeling our way down the stairs and around the bicycles lined up along the pathways. But the quality once inside the front door was okay.

The food was good – pleasantly simple (most meals seem to be made up of very complicated dishes with everything done in a variety of sauces), and I discovered my chopstick skill is such that I can pick up cherry tomatoes. Not an easy feat.

Back to sightseeing. On Tuesday (after packing an incredible amount of work and meetings and food into Monday and most of

Tuesday) I was taken to the Summer Palace by Mr Lu, a Beijing education officer. A man of some influence, so we were driven in a car which can use bus lanes, overtake where others can't, and drive into and around the grounds of the Summer Palace, which is a most wonderful peaceful area of lakes and walks, trees and flowering plants, bridges and beautiful buildings – the place where the Emperor and his family would go in the summer to escape from the heat. I gather for 'family' read 'concubines', but the Empress had a palace of her own, so maybe she didn't mind too much.

So we walked and admired, and every time we got out and walked for a bit, the car followed obediently behind and was there to pick us up. As most cars have tinted glass to keep out the sun (so the passenger can see out but to outsiders the windows are black) this had something of the atmosphere of a spy film. The party was made up of a local education official and his deputy, the head of a business college, Miss Li, myself, and a young woman (English name, Joanna) who was the interpreter, and for part of the time a Chinese colleague from England. However, he went back to Beijing to spend the night with his brother while the rest of us spent the night there. For all the world just like sleeping at Hampton Court – immense high rooms, beautiful furniture, rich coverings and carpets, ancient bathrooms – and all on an island in the middle of the lake (reached by a bridge), and the rooms were actually on the lake. Water lapping against the walls.

Quite incredibly beautiful and peaceful – and next morning we were up at 6 a.m. to go walking by the lake (again accompanied by the car, but now driven by the education officer – I guess the driver had a lie-in). We saw lots of mainly elderly people out doing morning exercises, which included ballroom dancing to an ancient tape recorder, and we all joined in. Miss Li commented that she had thought the English were cold, but was changing her opinion.

Breakfast, still in the Imperial apartments, and then a hurtling drive back to Beijing at 8.30 a.m. to start the working day, listening to light Western classical music. The 'Radestsky March' will always bring back memories of driving through Beijing traffic early in the morning. I had an appointment at a different university, but returned to a tough bargaining meeting at the Education Office later in the afternoon. Treats to the Summer Palace have to be paid for. (Their interest is initially to send school children to English universities from Beijing as China does not have enough university places, and then they are planning to set up a private senior school, specialising in language teaching, and they want our help.) We toured the building which is to be the school: impressive – over five floors – but of course no lift yet and no lighting, so quite a scramble. I was assisted round by the foreman. I guess he reckoned he was looking after the guest/old/woman/foreigner all rolled into one, so he was ultra attentive. Then when we left to go back to the tough bargaining meeting I saw him set off following the car on his bike; he arrived about five minutes after us, and presented me with a lovely rose plant in a beautiful pot. Of course I can't take a living plant back to England, so gave it to Miss Li. But it sticks out in my mind because so much of the kindness and hospitality (including gifts) are given to the position and have been arranged in advance, so anyone who turned up would be treated in that way. I felt the rose was given to me. Bet a foreman in England wouldn't be like that.

I'm getting very used to being the only foreigner 'yellow hair'. At the Great Wall someone asked me to pose with her for a photograph, and I am often aware of people looking at me. Of course I can't see myself, but I know that often I am half a head taller than everyone around me; I was the only European in sight at the Forbidden City, and the Ming Tombs, and in restaurants. Even in universities I am a somewhat rare being as the country really has not opened up yet. This is also apparent from the level of English. People who think they are good are very difficult to understand and have limited vocabulary and poor pronunciation, just through lack of practice. Public notices at tourist sites, put into English, are terribly translated and spelt. Although the hotel in Beijing was quite Western I could not find an English-language TV channel, or radio stations. And in Wuhan and Chengdu the lack of language ability in hotels, restaurants etc. (and the universities) is even more obvious.

Another airport – this time Beijing, where I am transferring en route from Chengdu to Qingdao. Qingdao is by the sea, so I've probably made a serious mistake in my planning by only having thirty-six hours there. 'The most beautiful city in China, and no pollution.' Now they tell me. We'll see. Mind you, so far I really have not seen any serious contenders in the beautiful city stakes.

Beijing airport, surprisingly, is not really very crowded. When I arrived I found a peaceful corner in the sunshine where buses and taxis were dropping people off, so I sat on my baggage trolley, leaning against my suitcase and wrote all my postcards. One joy I find in an overcrowded country is that you become anonymous. So in other places I might have felt self-conscious, but here I felt no one even noticed. And although there were occasional passing fumes from traffic, I think it was probably less polluted than many places I've been in. So having written all my cards, and successfully negotiated buying correct stamps – for France, Greece, Canada, America, Italy as well as England (what cosmopolitan friends I have!) – I decided to continue with this until check-in time.

The stay in Chengdu seemed to go well. For reasons going back into the mists of time, the university is one of eleven in China owned/run by the Railway Ministry. To be one of eleven (and the best of them) is significant when the alternative is being one of 1200 across the country. So it is reasonably well off, has money for visiting academics, and my timing was good as they are trying to move away from engineering, and expand languages, humanities, law and business studies. My room in the university hotel was a suite, with two balconies overlooking the university lake, flowers and fresh fruit daily. And, by day three, coffee for breakfast.

Apparently it is normal for universities to have hotels for visitors (and tourists which brings the university a profit). It is also normal for the university to be on a campus surrounded by a wall/fence and with security guards at both gates. It was the same in Wuhan. If you work or study at the university you live on campus; your children go to school there, there are shops, a hospital, and retired university employees continue living there until they die, with retirement clubs laid on. Rents are subsidised, and I get the impression that academics really don't have to do anything practical for themselves except a bit of washing and cleaning. Certainly no repairs, or gardening. I found it all a bit claustrophobic and insular, although it feels very safe and easy for visitors.

I was looked after by the Deputy Director of the International Office who is coming to England for a year. I went to her flat for dinner one evening – again drab outside but very well furnished inside, and relatively large. Three rooms plus living room, kitchen and bathroom, for her, her husband and their son. The son, aged seven, got very annoyed with me and asked me to 'talk Chinese' – I wish! But very odd; it felt very strange and far away, yet it was Saturday evening, and the seven-year-old was watching *Tom and Jerry* on telly, and his parents were telling him to eat up his food, or the telly would be turned off.

The next day I was taken sightseeing, to Qing Cheng Shan, a mountain which is the centre of the Taoist religion for the region. Very much a tourist area – but of course the tourists are Chinese. Then we went to a dam, Dujianyan, which was first constructed 2200 years ago, to control the floods and contain water to be used for irrigation. On the drive back to Chengdu, through miles of rural villages and small towns, I saw a working water buffalo.

Fortunately I also had a fair bit of time to relax in my suite, do some washing and sort my luggage. So by now I feel almost normal again, and kind of up to date, meaning I have sent twenty postcards, and sorted business cards, sent faxes to work, and caught up with writing my report of the trip.

Monday was a working day, with meetings starting with the university President and then various staff. It seems to have gone okay because the President was able to dine with me later (he had a diplomatic excuse lined up of possibly having other visitors, but then – after meeting me – found he was free).

After the President's dinner I had to give a lecture to the students, an occasion largely organised by the students themselves. Surprisingly, it was packed – definitely standing room only, but as it was scheduled for two hours they compromised and sat three people on two chairs, right around the hall. It went well – their understanding of English is good, and the hour I had allowed for questions stretched into one and a half hours, ending around 10 p.m. The questions included my views on Kosovo (tricky given China's opposition to NATO's action, and it became somewhat more interesting when they realised I felt able to criticise my own government), the merits of Eastern versus Western higher education, how you get a job in a country where the government does not arrange jobs for all graduates (this is changing in China, so students are interested in how we might prepare graduates for interviews, CV writing etc.), why we have visas, why are fees so high – and some very moving statements from some of them arguing that surely there should be free movement for education, so we could understand each other and make the world a better place. I could only agree.

So a lovely uplifting evening; just a pity that there was no obvious way of prolonging it by going for a drink. I think we could have talked all night but I was quite firmly taken back to the hotel. Maybe next time I will know how to handle such an occasion without causing offence but allowing for talking.

Well, time to check in. I am beginning to love airports. They are so peaceful, and I've had some sun.

Suddenly my trip is rapidly coming to a close, and today I am doing nothing more than relaxing at my hotel. It is on the outskirts of Shanghai (a city of sixteen million so the outskirts are pretty far flung) close to the airport. Called the Cypress Hotel, it certainly lives up to its name. It has grounds of about five acres, including a fishing lake, tennis and a golf driving range. It is a mixture of business and tourist hotel, and country club, belongs to a Japanese chain, and has both European and Chinese cuisine. I have absolutely nothing to do today so am taking full advantage of the hotel's grounds to lie in the sun, type this sitting under a cypress tree close to the fishing lake, listening to birds and traffic in the distance. It is also – of course – a chance to finalise some of my reports and thank you/follow-up letters for when I return to England. After sundown I will have to make use of the Business Centre, but not right now.

The thirty-six hours in Qingdao were fun. It is a beautiful city, or indeed series of cities in our terms, as it is so big (seven million plus), set along sea coastline with a series of beaches, which to us are complete bays, extending at least a kilometre in length each.

Unexpectedly it proved to be far more useful in a business sense than I had expected, so the day was busy, and I ended up having a working dinner at the hotel with the university's Director of International Programs. It is a very new university by Chinese standards – fifteen years old, with strong American and Australian influences. Although it is centred on a campus, many staff live elsewhere, and they have a lot of international students and staff. In a way the university reflects Qingdao itself, which feels quite Western: few bicycles (too hilly), very few Chinese style buildings, traffic which largely obeys the rules, and lots of Western/European restaurants, huge shopping malls, and so on. It is a holiday resort for the Chinese, and has one typical Chinese park, with a pagoda and quiet gardens, constructed in 1983 by the Qingdao tourist board.

A speciality of the region, exhibited in the pagoda, is miniature painting and engraving – for example, engraving on a human hair, which of course can only be seen through a magnifying glass; engraving on a needle, or on a tiny strip of paper which is threaded through the eye of a needle, to show 'six elephants pass through the eye of a needle'.

Part of the city was occupied/owned by the Germans at the turn of the century and this has left a strange European legacy of German-style solidly built houses, on wide avenues planted with trees, close to one of the beaches. Each one of eight avenues is planted with different trees, either types of pines and spruce, or cherry blossoms, which were just coming into bloom.

In these streets we came across a peculiarly Chinese custom – or current fashion trend. Newly married couples love to have their photo taken in Western wedding clothes. I gather they will normally get married in full Western regalia (rather than traditional Chinese red), at least in the cities. Dress, train, headdress – and the grooms in tailcoats of delicate pink, blue, yellow (rarely boring black or grey) with matching tie, flowers etc. On the wedding day itself there will be a lunch party, then the couple on their own, or maybe with one or two friends, will go to a beautiful spot (by the sea, or in these broad avenues) accompanied by photographer, assistant, make-up artist, and have studio portraits done. They will then return for an evening party with their guests.

If they cannot afford the photographer on the day itself, then they will save up, and some months later will have photos done. The outfits are usually hired for about £350 for everything – dress, suit, make-up, photographer. It has become such a fashionable thing to do that even couples who married some years ago will also hire the outfits and have photos done, often with their son or daughter included. Oh, yes – and to save costs on both sides the photographer will arrange to have about five couples to be photographed at the same time, picking early afternoon when the light is good. So you come across these batches of couples all being photographed, one after the other. The fishing lake at this hotel is clearly another favoured location. And the couples show no sign of being self-conscious. The first group I saw I assumed were fashion models for some advertising feature (and the men are more posey than the women. Certainly would outdo Italian males for swagger and assurance).

I left Qingdao very early, to catch an 8 a.m. flight, so came across another Chinese custom at about 6.15 a.m. Not only are elderly people out in the streets (well, on the pavements) exercising, but they bring their caged birds with them. So there are these little groups of elderly men and women (probably in their seventies and eighties – and no doubt some in their nineties) doing gentle exercises, and hanging in the trees around them are big, old-fashioned bird cages. I also saw them hurrying to get there, with their cages covered in cloths (one man with about eight cages on a bamboo pole across his shoulders). On reaching the spot, the covers are taken off the cages, so the birds can sing and enjoy the fresh air.

Shanghai is even more westernised than Qingdao – it's huge. I can't imagine living in a city of sixteen million. It must be divided into segments. The financial sector is made up of skyscrapers, huge buildings with reflective glass; the centre of the government is less imposing in height, but is spread over a large area, and includes a new opera house. I went to the Bund, an area of the foreign concessions alongside the river with strange European and American-style architecture from about 100 years ago.

I was also taken to Yu Gardens, a lovely haven of traditional Chinese styles in the centre of the old town (dating back several hundred years) and sat drinking tea overlooking a lake with a zigzag bridge. My guide was an enthusiastic lecturer from the language school I was visiting, who threatened to burst out into song when we visited the part of the garden where there is a stage.

1 May, Beijing

By Chinese standards, it was like coming home. Joanna and two of the officials from the Education Department were at the airport, and we had a happy relaxed lunch with far too much food – some was sent back and some put into doggy bags.

Then Joanna and I went sightseeing (Temple of Heaven) and shopping. Then… dinner at the Beijing Grand Hotel, overlooking Tiananmen Square – 'the Place to go in China'. For the fiftieth anniversary celebrations here in October a suite will cost 3000 US dollars a night, and visitors will have to book for a minimum of three nights. Miss Li arrived, plus a top official from the Ministry of Education, who was carrying twenty red roses for me (twenty is a lucky number in China). What an introduction and in what a location! All the other diners looked on in amazement. With people like that it is definitely love at first sight; the fact that he wants me to arrange for his unqualified 22-year-old son, who speaks very little English, to join a computing course in England has nothing to do with it.

Oh, and I forgot to mention – when I checked in at the hotel I had been 'upgraded to a suite'. They claimed that it was because the hotel was so busy, but I daresay the TV interview conducted last time I was here may have influenced it. Certainly I am treated extremely well. The suite is not only very luxurious – huge – but it is on the eleventh floor so has good views, and is very quiet, but I also get more items in the free tea and coffee selection, a very classy bathrobe, and fresh fruit daily. So instead of hotel breakfast I can lounge with coffee and fruit and give each day a leisurely start.

(This time in the departure lounge with my last Qingdao beer.)

Time to go home. I am longing to go home and see everyone, but I am also sad. Of course partly it is just the sheer ego trip of being treated so well (to think in England I will actually have to open my own car door and carry my own briefcase). But it is also leaving behind friends. There is always a special kind of intensity working across language and culture. On both sides we put 150% into communicating – eyes, gestures, extravagant facial expressions – so you cut through the conventions and seem to get to know the inner person deeply in a very short time. The most extraordinary example this time is my friendship with Miss Li. We are both desperately frustrated by the need to communicate, and yet a grin, a quick joke through the interpreter are enough. We have agreed to communicate by postcard – she also insists that I have her home number. I just have to ring, say, 'Nee how' (means 'Hello') and 'Sue', and she will get one of her sons to translate. Not sure I'll try it – yet I know she means it and that in Beijing I have a friend as tough and supportive as my friends in England who I have known for years.

The last three days here passed very fast. Saturday was a mixture of fun and work; the British Council handbook advises English visitors to be very careful with jokes 'particularly any with sexual innuendoes', but there was a lot of cheerful banter underlying the work.

Sunday was a heavy day. The Education Office had arranged for me to meet students who want to go to England and they, of course, turned up with parents. It was quite a formal occasion, very tense, and the students were disappointing in that they could not speak English well. Probably nervous, and the Chinese education system will focus on writing and grammar, not on talking. So I had to be tough and say that they would need to do a test we recognised – Grade A in their final year assessment was not enough. So that disappointment and the difficulty of explaining the intricacies of UCAS made it an uphill diplomatic struggle. We worked until about

12.45 p.m. – and although it was okay, I was mightily relieved when the same officials arrived to take me, Joanna and the office administrator for a late lunch and we resumed the banter and relaxed style. Obviously, the Chinese are not offended by my approach to the students, although worried about the level of English.

Then it was back to the office. I borrowed a computer to type up a fax to England, which allowed the Chinese to talk and then come back with questions – which went on until about 5.30 p.m. when wonderful Miss Li rescued me, complete with photos of the Summer Palace jaunt. So dinner, and then another meeting for me at the hotel, with senior members of a small college (the President apparently a former deputy Prime Minister). More explaining UCAS – they want to send students – and post-graduate university entrance arrangements. Finished about 10.30 p.m., retreat to suite and a well-earned glass of whisky.

The last day was spent partly with people from a government co-operative institute. I felt this was old China; they had real problems that I was on my own. This was not only unlikely for a woman, but also they seem to work in the world of lots of government money, and send delegations of about seven to do an initial meeting, then a further seven and then another group – over about two years, before a deal is struck. So we'll see what happens. They took me for lunch, and – horror of horrors – the first delicacy was goose head (I managed to be so clumsy with chopsticks I did not really engage in that one), followed by duck's head – but very spicy so I declined. The rest of the meal was okay, but I was glad to think I was going home tomorrow.

The afternoon was spent interviewing potential post-grads – at times quite frustrating until I realised with one or two it was not lack of English; they are simply thick!

And later, Joanna and others from the office came over, to check out final arrangements and share the last few hours together. Triumph: for the first time I succeeded in paying the bill.

They arranged a car to the airport with the office administrator so I had an English-speaking companion. I gave her the roses, so they have a few more days of giving pleasure. She told me about twenty being a lucky number. I think she was pleased – she clutched them all the way to the airport, and then insisted in accompanying me until the point where only ticket holders can go through.

Aeroplane. Good luck holds – three seats to myself again.

A few final thoughts: yes, it's true that the Chinese spit in public – but not all of them. Yes, it's crowded and polluted, although there are not the shanty towns of Indonesia or India, and, of course, no beggars. I am sure behind the surface I saw it is a very tough country. The one-child policy is rigorously enforced – not only no money to help with childcare but both parents are likely to lose their jobs if they have a second child. Many of the people of my age have two children (aged over nineteen) but those with a younger child will only have one. The young people I met seem to agree with the policy, and, of course, they don't miss what they've never had. I think they make close friendships through school – but that is also because, with only one child, parents do not really change their lifestyle as a couple. The child is looked after by grandparents (most couples delay having the child until they are in their thirties, thus delaying population growth, but it also means parents are likely to be retired), and the younger generation of parents continue a reasonably active social life around long working hours and few holidays. Of course I am generalising but am told that the main difference is between rural and urban China, and not between different levels of education in the cities.

My final thought? I hope I can go back.

See you all soon, with my photos!

Love, Sue

Early Days in Beijing – 2001

二
〇
〇
一

Dear Everyone,

I think (hope) I have been in contact with you all individually – by phone, by email, by postcard – so you know I am safe, that September 11 has not brought me back to England, and I am gradually settling in. But there is no way I can manage to tell you all about the life I am now leading – the fun, the excitement, and the challenges – individually. I will have to do these 'round robins', and send them by air or email. Of course they won't replace the more personal contact, the phone calls to family, but this way I can let you all know about this amazing world I am in, this 'awfully big adventure' I have embarked upon, without forever repeating myself.

So here is the first instalment about my life here – and already I've been here nearly a month, and I have so many impressions jumbling in my head. Writing them out may help to crystallise and sort them – just hope you aren't too bored. I had intended to get this off by the beginning of 1 October – National Day, so a holiday – but finding a computer where I can send an attachment is difficult.

I am having an evening in, because China are playing Oman in a World Cup qualifying match that China should win. If they do, they will qualify for the World Cup finals for the first time ever. So viewing is a *must* if I want to keep any credibility with the lads in the classes. It could prove to be a fund of English language possibilities. (They did win, and even if I had not been watching I would have known the result from the noise of firecrackers going off around Beijing. And in English Corner on Monday we learnt the new word 'nil' meaning the same as zero; somehow one-zero sounds all wrong.)

The last couple of days have included some real highlights. On Friday afternoon I stumbled across a gold mine of red wine from Australia and Europe (pricey but worth it for the occasional celebration); cheese, cheese and cheese; rye bread... and honey. I regret leaving the honey behind, but as I am not due to receive my first pay packet until Monday some discretion was necessary. I opted for a Chinese wine – very respectable and drinkable, but could not resist bread and cheese. Next door to this gold mine of Western food is an Italian restaurant which apparently is authentic in taste – so when Chinese food becomes too much I know of a reasonably priced alternative. Having ventured into the expat world the previous weekend I know that finding Western delights at a reasonable price is not easy. Lunch at a German-style café was £5 for a small quiche and a bowl of raw carrot. I am reliably informed that the expat salary is around £100,000 so £30 for a bottle of wine, and £100 for a meal is not stretching their budgets too far.

I am staggered to read the British Council reckon that £171 per day is the price in China for those taking part in a recruitment fair. Even if they spend £100 a night in an upmarket hotel (my hotel is £28 a night), to spend £70 a day takes some doing. Most meals out are less than £5 in Chinese restaurants; a taxi ride across Beijing is probably £2.50 maximum; internet use, even in the poshest hotels is only £5 per hour. By comparison a salary of £400 a month is average for a university lecturer; someone on £800 is regarded as well off.

But back to other delights of the weekend. On Saturday one of my students took me to the home of her grandparents (actually great uncle and aunt, but 'grandparents' is the term she uses; similarly 'cousins' become 'brothers' or 'sisters' – and in a way it is a good description because the family ties are so close). The grandparents, both eighty-one, have been married for fifty-eight years; the wedding portrait from 1943 is in a place of honour (and they are just about recognisable – she small and beautiful, in white; he, studious in glasses, in tails with a shining top hat under his arm). They live close to Tiananmen Square in a single-storey courtyard house (you go in through a door in the wall of the street, and then there is a small courtyard and single storey and single depth rooms all round). It is actually bigger than I expected. Going into one room which fills one side of the courtyard, you enter through a door in the middle of the side wall; ahead there is a single bed, lengthways along the outer wall, and a double bed, lengthways along the outer wall, plus heavy furniture at either end on the cross walls. So the room must be a good 15–18 feet in length. And the beds do not take up quite half the width. There is a desk on the outer wall to the left of the door; numerous single chairs; a coffee table and so on. Going into the room to the left, which forms the corner of the courtyard and then on to form the next side, again a corner settee and a double bed get lost against the outside walls and the corner. There is a telly (in fact two at least), a fridge/freezer, an air conditioning unit – and when you go through into the kitchen which leads off this corner room, still making up the second side, you find a microwave – as well as an old-fashioned cooker using the charcoal bricks I have seen being delivered to these type of houses. In the washroom/bathroom which leads off the kitchen I could see a Western-style WC (no, I didn't actually venture in) with running hot water, and a sense of light and airiness. This is partly because the house is reasonably well decorated with white emulsion, and good lighting. The third side is owned by the government and someone else occasionally lives there; and the fourth side is where the couple's third daughter lives, plus husband and eighteen-year-old son. I suspect the conditions are better than average, partly because this elderly couple are sometimes 'shown off' to visitors by the government. They have photos of visitors from Denmark and Sweden and a photo of members of a Scandinavian Royal Family. I don't think the Royals visited, but I gather that these visits come about because the government arrange them, so I assume the government approve of this couple and feel they do present a good face of China. The grandfather speaks reasonable English, having been educated at a church school as a child, which of course helps with the greeting of foreign visitors.

The other reason for the comparative comfort is – I think – because their family is reasonably successful. Their son, now thirty-six, has emigrated to Canada where he works as a doctor; the daughter who lives with them appears able to look after them full-time without needing paid work (and has a house elsewhere in Beijing, now mothballed while she looks after parents).

The family are lovely, very welcoming and I stayed for lunch. Simple, very good, and they kept on saying I was no trouble, 'Just an extra pair of chopsticks.' I hope to go back, especially when I can speak just a bit more Chinese to be able to communicate. It would be fun to go shopping and then cook with the third daughter, who seems extremely competent.

And the rest of Saturday was spent with one of our MBA graduates, now a 'small potato' in a large multi-national, but with some critical management jobs to do. He first took me to a big department store to look at things like washing machines, VCD players, and all the other things he feels are essential when I get a flat. Actually a washing machine at £90 does seem sensible. Not so sure about the need to have a 'family cinema' but I could have the whole works, huge screen, big speakers, video, VCD etc., for around £1400. Only computers at about £800 seem comparatively pricey.

We then went to a wonderful Chinese restaurant which specialises in dumplings, and had a dumpling banquet (set meal – huge and very tasty as you get a selection of every kind of dumpling – which costs £4 per head). And finally to front row seats in the Beijing Concert Hall, to hear the Beijing Children's and Young Women's Choir. Stunningly good, with a very charismatic conductor, an elderly Chinese professor, in tails and a very elegant stick. He has injured his back, so had to do a lot of conducting sitting down, but seemed to have such control that he barely needed to raise an eyebrow. His wife, very beautiful and elegant, was the accompanist – in a simple white dress – and occasionally their son, now in his twenties and studying music in Australia, took over conducting. The first half was Chinese music, the second half Western. One or two of the girls had exquisitely clear, pure voices, and sang solos without even an apparent tremble of nerves. The boys were surprising – not that it was a surprise that the younger ones were in shorts and short white socks but so were the older ones, whose voices have broken. Standing, apparently with no sense of being self-conscious, in navy shorts, short white socks, and red bow ties! Some sophistication crept in among the girls – some very bright red lipstick, and one, just one, who had a hint of glitter in her eyeshadow.

No technology to send you photos, so here are some Beijing snapshots in words:

The cyclist (1): sheer joy! A teenager (if it was England I would have said a sixth-former) in school uniform, with a drop handle racing bike – and a huge bouquet of white lilies. This was so big he had it tucked under his left arm, cradling it, and he rode, casually, with skill and panache, weaving his way, single-handed, between other bikes, buses, taxis, cars, with no sense of fear or nerves.

The cyclist (2): this time a student-aged boy (i.e. early twenties?) with a girl sitting side-saddle on the carrier behind him. Nothing so unusual in that, except that the girl had a guitar in her left hand, and her right arm was in a sling. Weaving their way through the Beijing traffic on a dual carriageway...

The cyclist (3): it is evening, and dark, and I am walking along when I hear someone talking behind me. I glance back, and there is a man on a bicycle, apparently talking to himself. But as he overtakes me, I see, perched on his crossbar, sheltered by his coat which hangs down loosely on either side, is a very small child, maybe under two. I guess he is talking to it to ensure it stays awake while they ride home together.

Dealing with blocked main drains. To get to a drain, of course, you need to lift the manhole cover – which, of course, is in the middle of the road. And it's about 8.30 a.m. So traffic everywhere. To deal with this, a group of men (volunteers or press-ganged?) go and form a ring around the manhole cover, and the cars just about steer round them. The cover is then lifted up, within the ring of men standing around it; whatever needs to be done is done, and the cover is – roughly – put back. But only roughly. Only part of the cover is in place, and the rest is sticking up. By now the men are in full retreat to the pavement – and it is left to the passing cars to force the cover properly into place.

Street fighting. No, not football hooligans, but two women, in the middle of the afternoon. I have no idea of the cause. It was just outside a supermarket, close to the main entrance, by the bicycle park. I crossed the road and arrived by chance at the scene, just as one of them (neatly dressed in tightish skirt and low heels) did a leap and kicked at the neck of the other (in trousers/tracksuit). Failing with this effort at kickboxing, she then removed one shoe and began to attack the other woman with the heel of her shoe, hitting as if it were a hammer. People were watching, and one or two tried to intervene – but it lasted maybe five to ten minutes. Certainly long enough for me to go in, buy some things, and come out to find it still going on. No one seemed to be badly hurt, and eventually the tight-skirted one got back on her bike and departed.

Spitting. Not as widespread as you might fear but nevertheless a feature of life. I have decided that you don't need to worry if you are close to an expert. You can easily identify them; they make a virtual aria of clearing chest cavities, lungs, rib cage, throat, tonsils, and only after a good couple of minutes of this activity are they ready to spit. Which they then do with confidence and accuracy, safely away from others. The less experienced, the tentative, the ones who maybe sense that this habit just might cause offence, are the ones to beware. Lacking confidence and certainty, the act of spitting lacks accuracy and force, and may well lack the necessary velocity to clear bystanders. Best to get clear first!

Demolition sites. Demolition is a 24-hour activity (as is much of the construction work here). Close outside my window I am watching a tall brick chimney being demolished. I am on the eleventh floor and the chimney was at least up to the sixth or seventh floor when at full height. The initial stages of demolition seem to have been carried out by a single workman, who climbed up to the top (possibly attached by a rope) then sat with his legs dangling down the chimney, knocking bricks off with a club hammer. This went on for a few days, with him gradually getting lower. Then, when it was still about three storeys high he climbed up, plus pneumatic drill. And he now uses that. Starting at 7 a.m. As the neighbouring building (apart from us, the hotel) is a hospital, I dread to think what his working hours might be if there was no consideration being shown to visitors or patients. He does not continue after dark. But the demolition does – within the building that is being demolished. Inside, so they have some light I guess. But through the night there is the regular sound of skips being filled, walls being knocked down, and rubble being shifted. I am told the legislation allows people to do a working day of eighteen hours.

Boredom. Not mine, although there are times when the hotel room gets claustrophobic, but the boredom of the lives of so many people here. Labour is cheap – and people work long hours in boring jobs, to earn very little. Restaurants can afford to have one or two 'meeters and greeters' – often dressed in a local costume or, young women dressed in pink, orange or pale lilac taffeta, looking for all the world like misplaced bridesmaids. These dresses are actually quite grubby when you look closely, but who looks closely as you go fast into a restaurant? These women are there from early morning until late, just standing opening and shutting a door.

And the people who work in the business centre here. The centre is open from 8.30 a.m. until 10 p.m., seven days a week, with the same group of four or five girls working there. They are bored, bored, bored. Hours go by with no clients. They do their nails, pluck each other's eyebrows, play patience on the computers, and talk on the phone (local calls are free in Beijing). And people working in shops, or small stalls on the pavement. Often they are asleep at the till or by the counter. One shopping centre nearby has about sixty people working in it and seems to be almost deserted. Yet day in, day out these people just sit there.

Pets, particularly dogs. This one is a surprise. Pets, particularly dogs, seem to be becoming popular, yet it costs 5,000 RMB (just under £500) for the first year's licence. And 2,000 RMB every year after that. Would people in England keep dogs if they had to pay that amount?

Expats. I must be careful on this one, because I too am an expat; I miss cheese, red wine, coffee, and I get frustrated by the thousands of trivial things which go wrong every day, and the never-ending bureaucracy. But one tale: the expat with the young Chinese wife, who talks of 'My last wife, a New Zealander.' He certainly has had at least a couple more before her, and now the Chinese wife is dismissed as a study machine. Just as a lawnmower is a machine for cutting grass, so she is a study machine. Expect her to cook? Hah! Would you expect a lawnmower to cook? I moved gently away from his sphere of influence and talked to Canadians.

With luck you will all now begin to feel some of the sheer fun and interest I have every day living here!

Sue

Dear All,

Season's greetings from a cold – but dry and sunny – Beijing. The sunshine and blue skies are a real bonus; my flat has an east-facing balcony which leads off the main room (well, the only room really!) and the days when I start work at a reasonable time I can enjoy some sunlight. Of course there are the other mornings (three of them) when I am at work before eight o'clock, and therefore leave in the dark. But it's not as bad as the life of many of my students, who are up at 5.30 to 6 a.m., and spend about an hour travelling, to get to college by about 7 a.m. – and then they clean the college!

I am sorry I have not been in touch very much over the last month – since I returned from England really. But life has become very busy. Not only is there a routine to my week with teaching commitments, two staff development sessions per week, and a certain amount of language support and advice for the teachers (who now know me, so are keen to ask for help), but I have also been accepted as an English Language examiner by the British Council. This is weekend work, quite fun and means I meet a lot of expats (Canadian, American, Australian, Irish rather more than English), but it does fill the weekend. There is invigilating on the Saturday morning (again an early start). The exam starts at 9 a.m. but there is about an hour's work, checking students' ID, and settling them in. Then in the afternoon and all day Sunday I conduct interviews to assess their level of spoken language – twenty minutes per student, and every examiner does about thirty per weekend. Each interview is recorded, and follows a set pattern, so it can become a bit tedious – but it is also interesting meeting and talking to the candidates. The demand for the language exam has rocketed, and of course at this time of year many of the examiners have gone home. So I have worked for the last three weekends out of four, and last weekend was flown to Shenyang (300 kilometres further north; midday temperature is about minus 15). Not that I really saw the city, or felt the cold. It was flat out work, and Saturday evening I spent in my (luxury) hotel room, marking and having a long, long soak in the bath. My flat only has a rather basic shower (yes, I do have running hot water, but only via the shower. Kitchen and washbasin are cold water only, which is why I say basic), so a weekend in a Holiday Inn at the British Council's expense is very welcome once in a while.

And of course the work continues over Christmas – or to put it another way, for me Monday is 24 December, Tuesday is 25 December and Wednesday is 26 December. Even the British Embassy and the British Council offices are only closing on Christmas Day. 1 January is a holiday, and the government has decreed that everyone can have another two days, 2 and 3 January, *but* to earn these must work on 29 and 30 December (i.e. the weekend). However, I am being allowed a long weekend, so will have about a week off. I think the Chinese also feel it is easier to have the various Chinese New Year parties using the Chinese language only, so I am being excused compulsory attendance to watch students singing Christmas carols and one or two other pop songs in bad English without music.

The big change in my life since I returned from England in late November is that I now have a flat, and it feels permanent. It is in a Chinese block, and to call it a flat is to be very polite. The whole floor area is about 10 yards by 4 yards (if you work in metres, then maybe 10 metres by 3.5 metres). You come in through a door at the west end (off a very grubby corridor, where the windows are always open – government instructions; it keeps us healthy to have fresh air). The hall is maybe 4 yards long, and less than 2 wide; with the kitchen off it, 3 yards in length and 2 yards wide; and the bathroom off it, which is possibly 1 by 2. Then you go into the main room, which is 5 by 4; and finally the balcony, which is 1 yard deep, and runs the full 4-yard width of the flat. In effect the 10 by 4 oblong is divided into one oblong of 4 by 4, which is hall, kitchen and bathroom then the main room and then the balcony.

It is warm, furnished, and I have a telly which gets one of the Chinese English-language channels – and relatively cheap (less than 200 pounds a month). Oh, yes, and I am on the ninth floor, fortunately close to the lift (which has an attendant, who sits there pushing buttons from 6 a.m. to midnight; there are three lift girls I think). Of course the lift is serviced every Monday, so that day you use the stairs. And I have my computer working, a land line (0086 10 6404 9308 if you want to ring, but remember my time is eight hours ahead!) and generally it feels like home. I even went to IKEA to buy a cafetière, notice board and one or two other useful bits to make life easier. The flat's location is brilliant, convenient for both jobs, and walking distance from a pedestrianised main shopping area, one or two of my favourite concert halls, and so on. And I have been approved by the Residents' Committee so should be allowed to settle. (Worth reminding myself, though, as I think of it as small, that many families – two parents and one child – live in this amount of accommodation, until the child leaves home in his/her twenties, to get married.)

I guess the other thing which makes life easier is I now can manage a bit of Chinese – with the lift girls, with taxi drivers, in shops. I am about to begin three classes a week which should mean I really make a bit of progress. I can even begin to 'read' some characters – reassuring when you are relying on taxi drivers, and you want to know where you are.

We have had one bout of really bad weather, when I was out for dinner way out in west Beijing, and the traffic virtually ground to a halt. I was lucky to get a taxi (the driver took sympathy on a stranded foreigner and also wanted to practise his English. We found out quite a lot about each other in pidgin English and Chinese). Interestingly the next day the snow was cleared by spraying warm salty water on the roads. Only the mix was a bit weak, so in parts of Beijing the roads became like skating rinks. Not good for buses – which adopted the tactic of getting all the passengers out to push.

So all in all, life continues to be fun and interesting. I have a lot of friends, including one or two really solid ones who make life that much more bearable (both Chinese and expats). I continue to feel very spoilt by many of my Chinese colleagues, and often have to tell 'white lies' to get time alone and to avoid being swamped by presents and items for the flat. I have the world's most hideous desk lamp (like an orange snail, and the base lights up as well as the light bulb), and also have a too-big Christmas tree, plus decorations, lights etc., brought round by one of my students and lovingly installed.

Anyway, must stop to email this before you all go off for Christmas. Be in touch again in the New Year; loads of Christmas wishes to everyone, and hope to see you in January, when I am back in the UK for nearly a month!

Love, Sue

Pause for Thought – 2002

二
〇
〇
二

(Written January/February 2002 while back in England for the Chinese New Year holiday)

It's impossible to pinpoint an actual day – or time – when I decided to go and work in Beijing. Looking back now it seems it was more of a process; for a long time I was wondering if this was something I would do, and then one day it seemed the decision had been taken and the move was happening.

I first went to China in April 1999, when I visited five cities over twenty-one days, as part of my work developing partnerships and recruiting students for an English university. I returned many times over the next eighteen months, gradually building a strong friendship and working relationship with Mr Lu, an education official in Beijing, and his senior colleagues. In November 2000 he was again asking me when I was coming back out to China, and I jokingly replied, 'I can only afford to come and work for you once I've retired; right now I need to work and build up my pension. If you were serious you'd offer me real money and a real job.' Six hours later he put a proposal to me. He was suggesting I go to Beijing and work as an advisor to two colleges, assisting with staff development, implementing changes in English language teaching so the students would become more confident and more prepared to speak English (not just read it), and changing the culture from one where the teachers traditionally have dominated to one where there is more respect for students.

All this was very exciting and flattering, but I was by no means certain I had really meant it when I had teasingly talked of going to work in Beijing. Would I be homesick? How would I cope with the lifestyle? What home comforts would I miss? What about friends and family? And, of course, what about my job back in England?

So there was a lot of talking to do, all of it prefaced with 'If' – 'If I go to China', 'If I let my house out to tenants', 'If I come back four times a year'… And then sometime around March it all seemed set. The university would agree to second me to work in China for two years, starting in September 2001. But even then it did not seem to be final. What if I didn't get a visa? What if I didn't clear the medical? What if the Chinese withdrew the offer? It must have been around May when it suddenly seemed as if the decision had been made ages ago, and I was on track to leave – and there were only three months left to get sorted.

Somehow everything did get done, including a lot of visits to friends to say goodbye. That was both good (I saw a lot of people I otherwise would not have seen) but also a bit disconcerting as it all seemed so final. But I know that China is only a ten-hour flight away; after all I have been going to and fro quite frequently for the past two years. So why, suddenly, was it so significant? Also lots of people gave me presents – which was lovely, but again seemed to be marking the event in a very definite way.

At the beginning of September I was off, packed, house let, furniture, books, pictures all lent out to understanding friends who offered to look after them for me while I was away. (Now, whenever I return to England, I visit friends and suddenly recognise something in their house, and remember it is mine! Very odd.)

The arrival in Beijing was quite normal. I was met by Joanna, my interpreter of many visits. She works for one of the Education offices in Beijing, and is really my right-hand person. Not only does she interpret, but she does a lot of other essentials such as arranging the payment of my phone bills (phone bills, both landline and mobile, are paid through the bank. Don't ask me why, they just are, and so are the electricity bills), sorting out hot water heaters, and the electricity in my flat, setting up my computer – and dealing with all the bureaucracy. I now have no less than three sets of ID: my British passport, a Chinese Foreign Expat's Certificate (which entitles me to a one year 'Z' visa) and my green residents' permit, which among other things entitles me to live in a Chinese housing area, rather than the expat housing. This means that my flat is cheap to rent and very convenient as it is very central, my neighbours are all Chinese, and all the shops are Chinese (although there is a branch of KFC about five minutes' walk away).

The most striking thing about my flat is that it is so small – really a bedsit with a very small kitchen and shower room attached. My bed is next to the desk with my computer, phone, family photos, and make-up on it; and then there is a sofa (sideways on) which fills the rest of the space. A huge wardrobe seems to take all my possessions – with enough space on top for suitcases and boxes. I have a small, very grubby balcony, which does for drying clothes, storing shoes and boots – and hopefully will have plants on when I return. It has been too cold over the winter, with the temperatures regularly below freezing. However, I chose the right winter: it has been unseasonably warm, two degrees above normal, and the pollution is now reduced so you can see blue skies every day. I can't believe how long it has been since I saw rain, probably two months of blue skies and sunshine with just the very occasional cloudy day.

One other, more basic point about my flat – I do have running hot water, but only via the shower. The water heater had to be installed, as running hot water is still not the norm for flats, and it is simplest just to fill the washing-up bowl from the shower rather than to try to have a second water heater installed in the kitchen. Some of my students will be living in small single-storey houses, along the *hutongs* (small lanes) in Beijing, without any washing or sanitation facilities, and they will use the communal washrooms sited along the streets. Oh, yes, and one other slight inconvenience: my washing machine is an old-fashioned twin-tub, rather like the one I used thirty years ago. I could get a fully automatic machine (and many do have them) but the question is, where would I put it? The twin-tub has to be lifted in and out to be filled from the shower, and if it stayed there all the time then I would have to stand on the twin-tub while showering…!

Having said all this, I am actually thoroughly enjoying living in Beijing. I am not homesick – although obviously occasions such as September 11 were not easy. But the Christmas period came and went as almost ordinary working days (I was teaching all that week as normal), and I spent the evening of Christmas Day with an American teacher and one of the university's Chinese MBA graduates who came over to drink English tea – his Christmas present to himself I think. Emails and easy phone contact home makes the distance seem quite small, and there are frequent visitors from England as well (all of whom have to bring me loads of newspapers and magazines). I can get English books and novels quite easily (although the Foreign Language Press mainly has eighteenth and nineteenth-century writers rather than more modern ones). There are Chinese television and radio channels broadcasting in English; as far as I could tell the information about the terrorist attacks and the war in Afghanistan was accurate and very similar to broadcasts in the West, but not so detailed or so dominating. China has other priorities – like the football team qualifying for the first time for the World Cup finals; the APEC meeting in November, when President Bush came to Shanghai; entry into WTO which was finalised in November. And, of course, the Olympics coming to Beijing in 2008, so even now the taxi drivers and police are focussing on learning English so they can look after China's guests.

One unexpected feature of China is that it is a very positive country; in a sense it reminds me of America. The GDP is steadily increasing by 8% plus per year; there is a firm belief in China's 'better and brighter future'; there is a confidence that China has a major role to play in world events, particularly now the country has entered WTO. There also is a certain amount of naivety – competition will work both ways; not only can China sell to more people and more countries, but also imported goods and imported foreign expertise could flood the country.

This confidence does impact on my daily life in a very direct way: my work is very focussed on new teaching methodology, motivating students, moving from a teaching environment to one where students learn, where there is interaction in the classroom. But if the students believe their future is bound to be better and brighter, then why bother to work? Interactive learning does require some input from them, and it is not always easy to see the value of this. It is hard, too, for the teachers to change, particularly when change can be seen to be threatening. Nevertheless I can already see some positive developments taking place, and it is this sense of satisfaction and purpose in my working life which adds to my enjoyment of living in Beijing.

Another unexpected feature of life is that most of my expat friends are not English, but Australian, or Canadian and a few Americans. Somehow I had thought I would meet and make friends with other English people, but in fact I have met relatively few, and many more Canadians and Australians. This does emphasise the different way I now look at the world; a world map bought in China has China at the centre, with Britain away in the top left-hand corner somewhere; news stories always lead on events in China and Asia; the weather reports barely touch on Europe (although I did hear about the snow in Greece at Christmas). None of this should be surprising, given that I live and work in Beijing, but it did take a bit of getting used to.

In some ways, being back in England is now harder than living in Beijing. I am writing this while I am back in England (it is the winter holiday in China, leading up to the Chinese New Year and Spring Festival in early February) and I am feeling at a bit of a loss. I have work to do, and meetings to set up at the university here, but it feels slightly odd as I will soon be going back to China. I have friends and relatives to see, and there is a lot of catching up to do… but it is also somewhat transient and temporary. There is an enormous gulf because my life is now so different, and China is almost more real than my former life in England. And then, even more disconcertingly, I relax, sink back, and it is as if I have never been away. Yet half my clothes, some of my favourite possessions, photographs, books, all remain in my flat in Beijing. I will return to them in a few weeks' time. I begin to think the answer is not to think of a life in Beijing and a life in Derby, but somehow to stitch the two together – but that may only be possible if more of my friends are able to visit me in Beijing (and hopefully some of my Chinese friends can come to England).

Living in China – 2002

二〇〇二

Dear Everybody,

New Year, New Job! And if you think it is a bit late to be saying 'New Year', well, maybe it is in the Western world, but here in Beijing we are just getting the new term underway. Chinese New Year was 12 February, but then there was the Festival of the Lanterns a fortnight later (coinciding with the full moon); term at the universities started today; at schools and colleges it started last Monday but in a rather sleepy, leisurely fashion.

And new job? Well, for those of you I haven't seen, or emailed recently, the news is that I have been 'promoted' to the position of associate or co-principal of a Languages College. I query the word 'promoted' as, to some extent, it is a questionable move. I lose much of the freedom of being an adviser, spending time between two colleges (with a certain amount of dillying and dallying on the way as I travelled from one to the other). The task is a serious one: the college has many problems which need to be addressed, urgently – not least we have more than fifty students due to graduate, supposedly going to university or technical college here in China or off to Germany. But nothing is in place to make this possible. We have to recruit for the autumn; the target is a recruitment intake of 150, but if we hit that figure we will need two more classrooms; another obvious problem is all my senior colleagues of course speak only Chinese. And while I am called 'associate', some of the local education officials seem to want me to take complete control, overruling the existing principal if I see fit!

On the other hand (the plus side), it is challenging, exciting, and already is proving to be fascinating. In many ways managing people is the same the whole world over, and not speaking the language is an advantage. I am not immediately aware of the undercurrents, or the internal politics – and am spared a lot of long, tedious meetings. There is little overt resentment, although a certain amount of quiet resistance under the surface – and a lot of things just don't happen. The challenge is to somehow bring in change, to update teaching methods, to get the students talking in other languages (and indeed studying in any language; many are pretty disaffected and have sublime confidence their parents will provide), to get the teachers re-motivated, confident and able to face change, particularly the advent of computers and technology.

I am also continuing to teach at a vocational school – twice a week, which is giving me the interesting experience of commuting across part of Beijing at lunchtime. The buses are almost empty, and many passengers are dozing; the traffic is light, and it is really quite pleasant. I also enjoy having time to myself, and avoiding the ritual of lunch. An apple as I travel is a welcome alternative to the institutional school dinners I would otherwise be having – and an English sandwich (made with excellent German bread, salami, cheese, and mustard!) is a feast.

Having been back to England for the winter holiday (aka the Spring Festival and the Chinese New Year), re-entry a couple of weeks ago was hard. It was not that I was desperate to be back in England, but rather that it was hard to really settle back here. I kept wondering what on earth I was doing – the first time I have really done that since I arrived in September. Not that England was that attractive – the wet windy weather was a major surprise to me – and I again was overwhelmed by the pressures of work in the West: the long hours, the bureaucracy, and meetings that seem to dominate UK education these days. Of course, little of this directly affected me, but I was very conscious of my freedom and autonomy in China, and the time I have here.

Whatever the reason for my difficulties in settling back, Beijing has done its best to comfort me. The days have been sunny and warm, and already it is daylight until 5.30 p.m. and beyond. I am woken by sunlight, coming in through the balcony windows, and by the time I leave for work the balcony is already warm. I have high hopes of growing some glamorous plants. The full moon was stunning, with sights like the Forbidden City (still adorned with extra lights from the New Year celebrations) and Tiananmen Square being quite breathtaking.

I also suspect some of my difficulty was just having to be back at work after a holiday (albeit with some work) back in England.

Anyway, I am now happily back, and last Thursday found myself actually looking forward to the next day, rather than just feeling neutral. A lot of this is just the enjoyment of the job. There is a lot to be done, but there are some very good moments. Last Thursday was good, because a group of four students came to see me, to show me a toy pig which squeaks if you push its nose – and we talked easily in French. This was all significant, because Chinese students are usually shy, and afraid of speaking, so to be so outgoing was amazing. And it was fun to be using French. My daily life does involve some French and even German as well as English and a smattering of Chinese, because the Languages College has a cohort of students doing French, another doing German, as well as a large group doing English. There is discussion about introducing Japanese next year.

Returning from England has made me see things differently. I am suddenly struck by how grubby everything is. I spent part of the weekend cleaning the flat, and am determined to get new curtains and a bedspread, to brighten it. I have also thrown out a lot of empty boxes left by the owner, and generally tried to impose some order. I am reminded of women's magazines from the 60s/70s with tips about living in a bedsit. I have bags hanging from coat hooks on the inside of the wardrobe doors, for socks and tights, to give me more shelf room. I will have to put winter clothes away in suitcases, and bring out summer clothes. An American friend is finding the same reactions; she says she has not only become compulsively tidy, but is also sweeping her room at least twice a day. Shoes need cleaning often, and my jewellery is literally filthy. It almost needs to be washed and then polished. And the dryness everywhere means I am again using creams and lotions several times a day. So different from England!

On the other hand, I am also finding it much easier living here. I know where to shop (and more bread shops are opening around me almost by the day; coffee shops which sell sickly cakes and buns are the latest fad); I am also more confident about trying Chinese vegetables, not worrying that I don't know the name, and have been buying meat from the butcher's in the Chinese supermarket. I have also brought back marmite, mustard and black pepper from England, so have some favourite flavours to hand. I have rejoined a health club at a nearby hotel, so can go swimming when I want, have a shower and sauna – all of which makes the flat rather more bearable. And I am constantly reminded of how convenient it is to live here. My interpreter/right-hand helper in the new job, Joanna, regards a one and a quarter hour journey to work as reasonable. Expats, living in luxury, secure apartments in compounds, pay a lot for the privilege and do not have the convenience of walking to work. Their local shops will charge expat prices while I shop alongside locals, paying stupid prices by Western standards. Last Tuesday, I was strolling back after a swim (strolling because it was about 14 degrees centigrade, so very pleasant for 9 p.m.) and I was able to buy China-grown strawberries off a cart on the pavement. About a kilo of fruit for 30p – and very delicious they were!

Something else that has struck me since I returned is that everyone in Beijing seems to be learning a language. The Westerners/foreigners are trying to get to grips with Chinese – many going to classes, and some taking regular exams. Apparently the numbers are increasing every year. At the same time all the Chinese are trying to learn or improve their English. So I practise my Chinese on the taxi driver, only to have him whip out a tape of English, or point to the glove box where his English textbook is waiting to be used whenever he is short of passengers. Joanna is preparing lists of sentences for her colleagues at the Education Office – 200 sentences for those over thirty, while the younger staff have to study for exams. Then, on the news this evening, I have just heard that people in Macau are learning Mandarin. Up to now they have spoken Cantonese or Portuguese, but now Macau is returned to China's mainland, they too are learning Mandarin – and even entering competitions to be the best.

Oh – one minor difference between China and England I keep forgetting to mention, but which is very significant on a daily basis until you get used to it: the floor numbering system is different from England – so that the ground floor is the first floor. My flat is on the ninth floor in China, but in England we would call it the eighth floor. Fine once you have got to grips with the difference – but then helpful Chinese, who know about the difference, will give you instructions using the English numbering system, but I use the Chinese… and confusion reigns again. Another quirk is the odd habit we have in England of answering a negative with a negative: 'You don't want anymore?' and we say 'No', whereas the Chinese answer 'Yes', meaning 'Yes, I don't want any more.'

At the weekend I went shopping with a Chinese friend – to Ladies Street, an area full of shops just selling women's clothes. A typical Chinese market, where you can bargain, and often they will offer to make you something if you don't see what you like. But, of course, the danger of shopping here is you feel so huge, so fat, so clumsy. Stall after stall with nothing in my size. Swimming is even worse; last week I had to cluck sympathetically with everyone else in the changing room as one tiny slip of a woman discovered she weighed 47.5 kilos. She seemed most upset by the 0.5, but I am sure she is vowing to get back to about 45 kilos now that the festival season is over.

So that's about it. Sorry this has been a bit work-dominated; more about China next time. I am now off to eat lettuce leaves and drink rice water, hoping to achieve the 45 kilos target which is a must for any self-respecting woman out here. Which reminds me of another oddity; many women drink hot water all the time – not tea, and certainly not coffee, but hot water. No wonder they are so thin. While the buses and underground are full of adverts for drinking milk because this will help to prevent osteoporosis. So there is the 'before' picture of a female silhouette with a very curved spine and humped back, and an 'after' picture of a female silhouette standing straight, with a gently curved spine. Very American in a way!

Loads of love to all, Sue

Dear All,

No, not an April Fool's joke. Instead I thought I'd tell you of a Chinese tradition carried out every Monday in every government school. On Monday morning at 9.45 a.m. all over China, there is the weekly flag-raising ceremony. So on Monday morning I too stand outside, while the students do some rather ragged marching and then, with due solemnity, raise the Chinese flag. Next, speeches. As the newly appointed co-principal of this government-sponsored languages college, I – of course – also have to make a speech. Something brief, explained simply (it will be translated, but if simple enough most of the students and some of the staff will understand anyway) which will herald the changes I am charged with implementing, yet will also both reassure and placate. The changes are not meant to be a criticism of what has gone before, but rather a necessary reaction to an ever faster-moving world.

In my last letter, I told you about my new job, which began with the start of term after the Chinese New Year holiday. As an associate head of a college it must be one of the most exciting jobs in education – and is certainly more fun (and maybe more challenging) than the world of further education in England.

Only of course I am not actually the head; I do not speak the language, I do not want to be involved in the day to day operational work, nor do I want to attend the inevitable interminable meetings at the Education Office. Rather, my role is to bring in change, particularly to the culture and atmosphere, to encourage independent learning, to stimulate the students to speak English/French/German rather than passively read, listen and occasionally write the foreign language.

I am working closely with teachers and students, assisted by an interpreter. As the college specialises in foreign languages alongside teaching the equivalent of the national curriculum, language is not quite the barrier it first might seem. I can draw upon French (A-level and beyond), or remnants of O-level German, together with a smattering of Chinese – as well as English.

Now, after only a few weeks in the job I am in no doubt that change is needed. The students are living in a culture which feels like the 1950s, yet at home they have easy access to the internet, to chat rooms, to pop culture. As far as I can gather their internet time is unsupervised, many chatting by email until the early hours. Then they have to get up at 5 a.m., to be on a bus to college by 6 a.m. The journey may be well over an hour, so they arrive around 7.30 a.m., for half an hour's 'reading' before lessons start at 8 a.m. The reading period is used for homework, language reading, tidying the classroom, and – for many – it is also breakfast time. They eat doughy-type rolls with a fried egg in the middle, or savoury, herb-flavoured folded pancakes, bought from local stalls just outside. They are supervised by their form teacher, reprimanded if they are not in uniform, given information about any changes for the day ahead, and generally the day begins in the somewhat scrappy, informal way that is the same the whole world over.

Formal lessons begin at 8 a.m., each period runs for forty-five minutes, with a ten-minute break in between. At 9.45 a.m. there is a half-hour break, used for flag-raising on Monday, and for formal exercise on other days. Lessons begin again with a five-minute eye-exercise routine (to music), a further two periods, and then lunch at 12.00. 'School dinners' are bought in from a nearby restaurant; hamburger-style polystyrene boxes with Chinese food, a separate one of rice, and rice porridge or soup. A Chinese version of fast food, with all the trappings; throw away the boxes, bowls and chopsticks after a single use. In some of the more environmentally friendly schools, students and staff use spoons, to reduce the amount of wood which is used for disposable chopsticks.

In the afternoon, which starts at 1 p.m., three more periods (and another set of eye exercises). The formal teaching day finishes at 3.40 p.m., and then the students set about cleaning the building – classrooms, corridors, toilets. This again seems to be standard across China. There may be additional classes, and then they embark on the long trek home – probably having a twelve-hour day with no free lessons, no private study time. Yet these are the equivalent of fifth and sixth form students aged 17, 18 or 19. The evening is food, homework, internet – and a certain amount of socialising with friends, if parents allow this (or presumably if parents don't know about it).

My task is to bring in Western-style management. Precisely what this is, is not clear. There is a view held by many here that Western education is better, that there is more respect both for students and teachers, and that students will learn better if respected and encouraged, not harangued and humiliated. I have no doubt that this is true – but translating ideals into reality when I do not have the necessary language skills (although I do have an excellent interpreter/assistant), and am viewed with a certain amount of suspicion, will inevitably be challenging.

There is a lot to be done. Traditionally Chinese students sit in rows in large classes (classes of over forty even for language teaching are not uncommon). Students are separated, sitting in single lines of desks to prevent any talking or communicating. Teachers stand at the front and lecture (or in some cases even sit at the front, and cannot be seen by students at the back). Use of the blackboard is not that common, and teachers rarely walk about. Textbooks are old – or if new are, in fact, a new edition of an old text. So one of the oral language books I see in current use portrays an England where to make a phone call you use the operator, where doctors come out to visit a sick teenager with a headache, where women do not work and afternoon tea is usual. I constantly have to shatter illusions by explaining the reality!

Another aspect of my work is to improve the language teaching, not only of English, but also of French and German, to find authentic teaching materials, to develop contacts with the embassies, with any other schools teaching these languages, and to get rather basic display information such as maps. Of course I am assisted in this by the teachers, but the German teachers are Chinese who have not had the chance to travel outside China and the French teachers are in a similar position. So although their command of the language is good, of course they are reluctant to put it to the test with native speakers. Nor do they expect to have a say in the choice of teaching materials. Traditionally this has been done by the education committee, or the school senior management. Teachers do not feel confident to do this, and as most of them are paid on an hourly basis, would actually say that they are not paid to go looking through materials and selecting the best. They are paid for the time they are physically in front of the class.

Getting back to basics: a school cleaned by the students is not exactly a clean school, so I am beginning by getting a classroom cleaner, and making the school safer. Odd loose electric cables must be pinned back; outstanding small repairs must be done. I am equipping myself with a pleasant, efficient office, with computer and internet connections, a phone and a small meeting table (bought from IKEA – definitely breaking the Chinese formal government mould). My theory is that if we get the school cleaner and tidier, with some attractive displays on the walls, even notices in four languages (Chinese, English, French and German), we will begin to have a better environment in which to work, so we will all be happier, and more motivated – and maybe this will rub off on the students. Developments in teaching methodology, modernising materials, even changes in staffing will take a bit longer.

So an exciting new job – but there is a long way to go. Happy April Fool's Day!

Love, Sue

Dear Everyone,

It's eight o'clock on Sunday morning, and soon I have to get dressed and go out to the British Council Education Exhibition at the China World Hotel, behind the China World Trade Centre. Yes, Beijing too has a World Trade Centre. The Education Exhibition is a way of recruiting students, although legally we are not supposed to give out application forms or make offers to students during the exhibition. This is not allowed as the Council has permission from the Beijing authorities for an international event, but that does not include active recruitment. The reality is a large conference hall, set up with booths for various universities and colleges, crowded out with potential students. Literally thousands will attend over the two days; last time 40,000 potential students attended in a day and a half. So it is hot, crowded, tiring and frustrating because of language problems and the huge lack of understanding of higher education among the young Chinese. So many just want a Master's without any idea that it requires a first degree, with no idea of which subject they want to study (or would be qualified to study) and with unrealistic ambitions about the level of language they have, or will need, in order to study. Luckily I'm not on my own; staff from the International Office at the university have flown out for the occasion – and we have also had assistance from some of our Chinese graduates, which helps with the language problem.

I am beginning, gradually, to understand the reasons for this ignorance and the sense that education will lead to prosperity – any education, so long as it is Western. China's education history is short; in the late 1950s it was a high point when 60% of the population went to primary school. And many of these would only go sporadically, perhaps once or twice a week, and only at certain times of the year when there was no work to be done on the family's land. Compared with England, where we all went to school, I can immediately sense how short the memory of education is in China. There is so little history of education at family level so almost nothing to build on.

Young people in their twenties today will have grandparents who cannot read; some talk of grandmothers who have so little education and language that they cannot follow soap operas on television. And of course parents with a university education are rare, not only because of lack of provision, but also because of the huge impact of the Cultural Revolution which affected all those in their late teens to early twenties between 1966 and 1976. The contrast between the tightening up and control, restrictions on books, on knowledge, and on travel happening here in China (not to mention the exposure to violence which must have been widespread), and the sixties' generation in the West is immeasurable. Those who did make it into higher education in China then did not choose the careers they followed; they were allocated jobs. This seems to have continued until quite recently. So I cannot appeal to the better nature of many of the teachers I manage, or ask them to think why they came into teaching – they didn't choose this career; it was given to them.

Yes, well, the long silence is explained by the crowds who attended the Education Exhibition – we were almost mobbed. At times during the day we had four or five students at a time filling out application forms, crouched down behind our stand, because we were repeatedly being told we were not supposed to be collecting applications, just giving information. And although other stands were busy, the combination on our stand of a foreigner who is working in Beijing and a young, very English-looking male who spoke Mandarin was obviously a major draw (and helped a number of waverers actually make a decision).

For the next two weeks my evenings were taken up with more applicants, meeting young people in various hotel lobbies and various branches of Starbucks, to discuss their career choices and guide them forward.

The saddest story is of two young girls whose parents took them out of school at fourteen, and sent them to do GCSE in England, at a private boarding school. After four terms, as GCSE approached the girls realised that GCSE did not give them direct admission to university, so they ran away from school and returned to China. They were then put on an intensive English course here in Beijing, and then that autumn sent back to England. This time one of them went to do A-levels (Maths, Biology and Business, I think) and the other was accepted on to a pre-university foundation programme. But again they ran away after two terms, and returned to China. So they are now about seventeen, without any structured education in the last three years. They are fluent in English, because as well as studying in England they have also been working part-time, but they have no chance of re-entering any public education here in China, and their parents have experienced a real loss of face. The parents seem to have limitless amounts of money, but not a lot else.

I had a brief trip back to England over the May holiday, (carrying lots of application forms with me) and am now back in a rather warm, sultry Beijing. I am typing this at 10 p.m., but I think it is still about 18 degrees outside – fortunately there is a breeze, and as I am on the ninth floor it is quite refreshing.

Beijing is transformed in the hot weather – pavements become full of people sitting outside most of the day. They will be playing cards, or mahjong, or Chinese chess; many will be sleeping (today I passed one young man asleep in a hammock, slung between two trees), and others just chatting. But even though it is hot I notice there are still some locals who are reluctant to shed their thermals, and as I was melting in the heat at lunchtime (around 25 degrees) I passed a group of youngsters all in tracksuits, wandering along, zipped up to keep warm. I now shut my kitchen door if I am cooking, because the kitchen gets so hot I don't want that heat in the rest of the flat. I have turned the water heater off in the bathroom and only turn it on about every third day when the water becomes tepid. Keeping it on all the time just makes the bathroom too hot. Yes, I do have air conditioning, but I am saving that for the hotter weather (and anyway I don't have a lot of confidence in it, because I have one broken window and none of the others fit well).

My Chinese language skills progress slowly. Returning to England was probably not a good idea, and my teacher is now cramming for accountancy exams, so lessons have temporarily halted. But I now say, 'I want to go to…' instead of just saying the place name to a taxi driver; strangers in the lift ask me my age (that is not considered rude in China, just normal, along with questions about salary), if I have children, and today I was told I looked healthy. Not sure if I do, just hot and tanned, but I was very chuffed that I understood. Counting, numbers, telling the time, is all much easier.

Work is definitely not easier. There is talk of the college where I am co-principal being merged with another bigger school, which is unsettling. I am told I will have a similar job to do – but don't actually know where this other school is! We are very much in need of students for next year, but have not started recruiting any yet; we need good teachers, but have just sacked one, and threatened two trainees with the sack if they don't study hard. I have to take responsibility for this, given my position – but of course I don't officially get told what is happening until days after it has happened – by which time I know anyway.

On the other hand, the other school where I teach and do some training of the teachers is really enjoyable. My students are now fluent enough in English to make teaching – or at least communicating – easy. The intention is that they will come to England to do a Business Studies HND in September 2003. One of them has just told me he is running a shoe-selling business with a friend in his spare time, and has already made more than $90 profit in two weeks. Bearing in mind that the average Chinese salary is $900 per year, this is good going. Does he really need a degree?

Oh – I have had my first parents' evening in China. In the college it was all a bit surreal, because there is nowhere big enough for all the parents to gather together. Instead they arrive and go and sit in their child's desk, in the appropriate classroom. The head teacher then addresses them over the loudspeaker system – and he went on for nearly an hour, including reading out lists of names and exam results. So you have these parents looking awkward sitting at a slightly too small desk (and if both parents attend, then one has to stand) with the head teacher's disembodied voice booming out over a very crackly and distorting tannoy system. He and I then did a tour of the classrooms, and met with some hot, grumpy parents, who clearly felt they deserved better treatment. Very different from England.

Outside of work, I am much better organised, knowing where to shop for Western food (happiness is finishing a long Saturday of invigilating and then examining for the British Council, and going home knowing I have red wine, cheese, butter, bread – and even bacon for a bacon sandwich before I go examining on Sunday), where to go for books, how to bargain for clothes – and generally knowing my way around. I can phone home very cheaply. It used to be £10 for half an hour using a phone card, but I now have a legitimate source of phone cards at half price, so it only costs £5 for half an hour.

I am also reviving my determination to enjoy living in a big city, and take advantage of all the opportunities. So I have a ticket to see the RSC in *The Merchant of Venice* this week; I went to Mozart's *Requiem* at Easter, and have just discovered free French films with English subtitles at the French Lycée. I am also playing truant one afternoon to go to a demonstration of Chinese painting and calligraphy.

I have a well-established group of friends out here – Chinese, Australian, Canadian, American, Chilean, an Albanian, French – and even one or two English. Most are teachers, or in some way linked to education, and they have a huge mixture of backgrounds – ex-Peace Corps, ex-backpacker, graduates of Chinese, people who have lived through Mongolian winters in tents with outside temperatures of minus 35. Apparently once it gets below minus 20 it really makes little difference – 'Your scarf is frozen to your face, and can't freeze any more.'

One interesting post-September 11 comment from an American/German who lives in southern China. He uses his German European Union passport almost all the time, rather than his American one. He is accepted more readily in Asia as a European, and reckons he does more business, and of course he can travel freely around Europe, and work in so many countries.

I am having quite a lot of chances to travel – mainly with the British Council for examining at weekends, but occasionally to visit schools looking for links to England and English universities. About a month ago I went to Nanjing (two hours flying south), and then a three-hour car drive to Taizhou, Jiang Zemin's birthplace. The countryside is very different – lush, green, rich, very fertile – and the houses all well spaced out with an air of prosperity. I suspect that life is relatively financially comfortable, but hard work and boring, with little opportunity for education, and those who do get away, stay away. (Rather like rural life everywhere – seemingly attractive, but the young people move away.)

The school is a large boarding school, private, funded by local businesses, and already very popular although it was only opened in September. Many of the children don't need to board as they live nearby, but boarding is compulsory so that schooling can go on all the time. It is very pressured and intense, with the carrot of a place at a university in China held out as the prize. As this is China, of course the 'meeting' began with a huge lunch, dish after dish of delicious, typical southern China food. And then the surprise – hamburgers from the local KFC, served in their polystyrene boxes but as they had been brought in about an hour earlier they were cold. But they were so happy to have provided me with Western food, complete with plastic fork and ketchup, I had to try to eat it.

We then drove to the local four-star hotel, where I was to stay overnight; we checked in, and had a sleep (from about 1.30 to 3.30 p.m.), me in my room, and the rest, seven Chinese men, in another room. At 3.30 p.m. the meeting really began – and was held in my room, sitting on two uncomfortable bedroom chairs, the dressing table stool, and the beds. At 5.30 p.m. the obligatory banquet, downstairs in the hotel – and then without warning, at 8 p.m., a television interview. Happily I left the hotel at the crack of dawn next morning, so have not had to see the TV programme.

So that's it for now – I'll email this and then try to get some sleep as it is getting cooler. I never thought I'd miss rain – and that wonderful smell after rain. I have a lot of plants on my balcony, and having watered them I stand there enjoying the smell of damp greenery and wet soil. I'll be missing mowing the lawn next.

Love to all, Sue

21 June

Dear Everyone,

Well, suddenly the first year here in China is almost over – and it will end unexpectedly soon. Having been holding a ticket to return to London on 16 July, (which was beginning to feel like a long time, particularly because of the heat here in Beijing), suddenly I am flying to Paris (yes, Paris!) on 8 July, and then on by train to spend a few days in Toulouse developing links there on behalf of the Chinese. Then I return to Paris and home for seven weeks! This Paris trip is a real bonus. I keep having to pinch myself to believe it is real. And the idea of representing the Chinese to build links at the university where I was a visiting professor more than ten years ago gives a wonderful twist to everything, and yet there is also the sense of completing a circle. It was the opportunity to go to France some years ago which made me decide to qualify to teach English as a foreign language; and now I am in Beijing using those qualifications.

I cannot pretend to be sad to be leaving Beijing – but of course I am coming back. If not, I definitely would be sad, not only to be leaving friends and places I have only just discovered, but also because the work here is not done yet.

Beijing in the summer is a tough city. The daily temperature hovers around 30 degrees centigrade – or rather the nightly temperature. The day temperatures go to the mid and occasionally the upper 30s. Yes, we have air conditioning; yes, we have manufactured rain, and also some amazing thunderstorms – but very little breeze, and not a lot of relief. It is not so bad when the days are clear, so the sun is really hot, yet you can breathe. So many days are heavy and oppressive with cloud. I cannot see the mountains on the edge of Beijing from my flat; on a clear day they stand out. The dust is everywhere – a thin, pinkish layer. Students are reluctant to learn, constantly fanning themselves and wiping their faces with their tee-shirts throughout the lessons. My sympathies are with them; I am meltingly hot too, but somehow we have to get through an hour and a half of learning English in the dead periods after lunch. We play games, do group work, do exercises – anything to break the monotony and somehow maintain concentration. Educationally I cannot believe that a term which begins in late February and lasts until mid-July with only a week's break in May makes any sense at all. Even worse, the crucial life-determining exams have still to be held. University entrance exams for Grade 3 students, which decide their future, will take place on 8 July; and the National Standard exams for the Grade 2 students are taking place now.

The university entrance exams are so important that parents book rooms in hotels so their child has a cool place to study and sleep; I have friends who have rented a second home close to their child's school for the month leading up to the exams to cut the child's travelling time each day, and, of course, most mothers will take holiday to cook and generally care for their child over this stressful time. The results rank the students; the top ones – nationally – will get to the top universities and study the course of their choice; slip a few points and you may end up not being able to study in Beijing, and not doing your chosen degree.

My flat does have air conditioning, and so far I've suffered no power cuts. But the window glass does not fit well, the air conditioning is noisy (and expensive in electricity) so often I keep cool with the through draught of having doors and windows open. The benefit of being on the ninth floor is a slight breeze almost all the time. Usually I fall asleep on top of the bed, and on a good night I will wake about 3 a.m. to cover myself with a very light sheet.

Many shops do have air conditioning, but my local supermarket doesn't – so I find I now rarely shop there. It is really oppressive and the mingled smell of different foodstuffs does not inspire me to buy anything. Instead I go further afield, to air-conditioned and refrigerated supermarkets, paying more and going back into Western style food – bacon, sausages, cheese, even frozen chips.

But life is not all work. Last weekend I was due to examine for the British Council in Xi'an, so I took a day off and flew there a day early – and spent Friday being a tourist. Of course I went to see the Terracotta Warriors and the factory which makes the genuine fakes, as opposed to the fake fakes made by the farmers or local peasants. You can tell a fake fake; it is made out of mud rather than terracotta and the mud washes away in the rain. A genuine fake will 'ping' when you flick your finger against it. The site of the warriors is amazing, as is the sheer conceit of an emperor who first thought he would have real people buried to protect him, and then settled for these models. I found I was left wondering what else is buried across China, and indeed across the world. The wealth and resources which must have gone into constructing this vast tomb and its surroundings are overwhelming.

Our tour also included a visit to hot springs and a Neolithic village which ran along matriarchal lines. The women inherited; a woman would have one husband who lived with her, but was free to have as many lovers as she wanted; children did not know who their father was – it didn't matter as they would not inherit through him. Adult cemeteries were on the outskirts of the village, but the bodies of children who died young were placed in urns, and the urns were buried either within the walls of the house, or very nearby. Before burial, holes were made in the top of the urn, so the child's spirit could slip out and visit its parents, and then return to the body.

Being among tourists, and being looked after, was sheer luxury. We were a mixed group – two from England, two Japanese, four Americans and three young Germans, including a German backpacker (his description of himself) who was backpacking around China by plane and staying in luxury hotels. A new definition of the phrase.

No letter covering the last couple of weeks could be complete without reference to the World Cup. It dominated the afternoons and evenings of early June because of China's involvement. For their first game, classes were cancelled (or televisions brought into schools), huge screens were put up in parks, restaurants, cafés – and of course Beijing's famous bar street was full of open-air screens. Small corner stores had TVs outside, and throughout the qualifying rounds a small group of men congregated on the corner of my block of flats, complete with telly (and a very long lead going in through some window to the nearest socket) so they could watch together. If you were out in Beijing while a game was being played, then taxis were mainly being driven by women. But it was all very good-humoured and relaxed. At my college the students had a competition of guessing the score in China's match against Brazil, with Parker rollerball pens (genuine fakes I think, not fake fakes – but certainly not the real thing) being handed over to the winners; nine of them guessed a 4–0 defeat.

A little bit more about work, and why I say there is still a lot to do. Part of my remit is to bring in Western-style management, and one of the catchphrases of management is 'communicate, communicate, communicate'. I've always thought there was a lot to be said for that approach, but now I am in a culture where the concept is not understood at all – and the consequent confusion, low morale, reliance on gossip and general rumour-mongering is amazing to behold. I am told, officially, that the Languages College, where I am co-principal is to merge with another nearby school. (This in itself is worth commenting on; the merger is necessary because the demographic consequence of the single-child policy, brought in twenty-four years ago and quite rigidly enforced in the city, is that there are fewer children and so fewer schools are needed now, and fewer still in the future.)

But back to the merger. I was told about it, and then I discovered that potential parents were going to be told because of the impact this would have on recruitment. So I suggested that we really should tell the teachers, as it was not best management practice for them to read about a merger in an advert in the newspaper, or via recruitment meetings. So it was then officially announced – but only at the Languages College, not at the other school. This other school is part of the same education district, so numerous meetings are being held to decide which head teacher will retire, who will do what, how we deal with redundant teachers. I am assured my job is safe, and I will have more responsibility for the language teaching. I then ask if I can visit the other site, as the plan is we will all move onto their site (bigger than ours). I want to look at resources, particularly the computers, as we are now doing a lot of computer-aided language learning. But this meets with a (gentle) refusal. First I am told the teachers there do not know of the merger so my presence would be a problem. And now, a month after the merger has been made official at the college, I am suddenly told that actually the merger may not happen – but I am not to say this to our teachers.

Meanwhile our recruitment is low, so we don't actually know how many teachers we will need next year; I have broken the mould by doing forward planning and actually deciding who will teach next year's Grade 3, Grade 2 and probably Grade 1 (provided of course we have enough Grade 1 students). We have also gone ahead and chosen new textbooks, and begun planning. After all term ends in three weeks, everyone will disperse so if we don't plan now it will be chaos in the autumn. But I seem to be the only one who is concerned. The teachers do seem to appreciate the forward planning, but are also a bit nonplussed. The majority are actually on part-time contracts, so they can leave – or be given notice – almost at the end of a week. I think many will not be paid over the holidays. I understand one of the deputy principals, who is in charge of all the academic work and does the timetabling, is due to retire at the end of June – but I am not sure who will take over. But again I seem to be the only one asking the questions. Joanna, my interpreter/assistant, busily goes off to try to get answers, and frequently returns with the reply, 'They haven't thought about it.'

This lack of communication is not confined to this one school, nor to education. Time and again foreigners (i.e. Westerners, expats) complain that we have to cancel one meeting or go to another at very short notice. The various national holidays and the official days off are only announced at very short notice – like a week before. Parents' meetings, the national examinations, concerts and theatre performances all seem to happen, and you find out somehow. When Joanna came with me to the Forbidden City Concert Hall (probably the classiest in Beijing) she was surprised that they had a poster with all the forthcoming concerts for the next six months. She was so impressed she took one away with her. Last week I went to a stunning performance of *Swan Lake*, performed by the Moscow State Ballet – but according to adverts and posters the performance was on one night only. It was thanks to Joanna that I found out it was on for a week, so could find a free evening to go!

Anyway, enough. I am finishing this while watching the Senegal/Turkey quarter final of the World Cup. This afternoon I didn't need to be told the result of the Korea/Spain match. I was examining at the Foreign Languages and Culture University, which has a lot of foreign students from Korea, and they made their delight clear to all by putting on a drumming display. Today has been cooler – the low 20s, with rain and a breeze. In fact, almost cold. If it's like this tomorrow I will definitely be Chinese and wear trousers to keep warm.

With luck I will be seeing a lot of you before too long, during my seven-week return to Europe – and maybe some of you will be able to come and visit me next year. If you are thinking of doing so, please get making plans, as I probably will not be living here the year after. I hope to keep the links into China, but probably reverse the time arrangement and be nine months in the UK and only three months out here. So get saving and planning. China is very cheap once you are here, and I can lay on free local tour guides as all my students love the opportunity to practise their English.

Love to all, Sue

PS: As it is cool this evening I finished this and then moved on to my ironing. The joy of ironing when you don't give yourself an ironing-induced sauna at the same time! And ironing reminded me of my great purchase. I am the proud owner of a brand new twin-tub washing machine. It cost about £40 (and wasn't the cheapest). Bought for cash, delivered the next day, and now I have really clean clothes, because the wash tub actually washes (the old twin-tub merely soaked the clothes) before using the spin side. Of course the palaver of lifting the machine into the bathroom and filling it from the shower remains unchanged, and there is nowhere to plumb in an automatic. So I have gone back thirty years, and love my twin-tub. The sense of satisfaction of having a row of 'whites' hanging on the balcony has to be personally experienced to be fully appreciated. This is China.

Dear All,

Well, I seem to have cracked the art of crowding into a Chinese lift at last. Today, with no problems or awkwardness I was in a lift with six other people and two bicycles. The lift is less than 1 metre by 2 metres, and also includes a stool for the lift girl to sit on. The key to all of this is to put the bicycles in at an angle – and as the lift stops at various floors as we go down, and picks up first one and then the second bike, everyone on the door side of the first bike has to get out, let the second bike in so it is tightly up against the first (parallel to it) and then we all get back in. A skill to be learnt when you live in a large apartment block on the ninth floor, in an area where bicycles are stolen so if you own a bike you bring it up in the lift and keep it inside your front door.

I don't have a bike, nor do I have any ambitions to own or ride one in Beijing. Life is complicated enough without having to worry about the rules of bike riding, whether your bike will get stolen, punctures (frequent as the road surfaces are poor), keeping vaguely clean (difficult as the roads are so dusty, and worse when it rains), finding somewhere to park your bike (often on the pavement in a kind of bike park, with an elderly Chinese woman guarding it – you have to pay for this, about 5p), not to mention traffic police. Actually I don't think they are police exactly, more like the equivalent of traffic wardens – civilians equipped with tie-on luminous overshirts (like the numbers that athletes used to wear in competitions) as uniform, plus whistles and flags. At every junction there will be at least four such people, who whistle and point furiously at bicycles. This may be to say 'move on', or 'you can go, filter right', but seems just as likely to mean 'stop, you are a foreigner' or 'stop, I want to inspect your papers' or 'stop, the route is now changed and you cannot go down here anymore'.

Many foreigners do ride bikes here, and seem to cope. I am told it is a good way to see Beijing (I can believe that) as it is slow, you become part of the group weaving along, and it is quite cool as you create your own breeze. Occasionally I am tempted but then reality steps in and I just feel it is a bridge too far. Of course others think I am mad using the buses (boneshakers was a word invented for Beijing buses), crowded, dirty, slow – but very cheap, many of them and they go all over Beijing. Once you know the routes you really do have freedom of the city. I also use the subway – also dirty, crowded, but cheap. It doesn't go all over the city – at present there is one loop line and one running east/west – but for the places it does go to it is fast and efficient, and a standard fare of around 20p. Also the underground stations have fantastic shops (well, market stalls or booths) selling clothes, shoes, bags, jewellery, accessories. A teenage girl's paradise as everything is so garish, but definitely high fashion, and the prices start low and can be bargained lower.

I also use taxis. This again marks me out as mad to the cyclists. To them, taxi drivers are cheats and very poor drivers. I have not had many bad experiences. The taxis all have meters and normally put them on as a matter of routine. I guess in the early days I was taken on longer than needed routes from A to B, but now I know Beijing this doesn't seem to happen. The taxi drivers' driving is a little unusual on occasion, but the taxis are so battered and elderly they really do not go at any great speed. A bit like dodgems at the fairground. I have not – yet – been in any kind of collision; somehow the taxis *just* manage to avoid each other and the other cars. I am sure that will change as the roads get more crowded and the average speed increases.

The taxis are also small – you can just sit one person in the front, but only if that person has very little luggage (a briefcase presents a problem), and two in the back. The rear offside door is normally locked, so both back-seat passengers have to get in on the nearside, and the first one in has to slide across. Knee room is almost non-existent, particularly if you get a 1.20 (this relates to the charge in RMB per kilometre). 10 RMB (less than £1) is the basic fare, and once you have used up that amount of metered travel, then additional distance or time is metered at 1.20 a unit. The larger cabs will be 1.60 (Citroën ZXs, and the 1.20s are called Xiali) and all of these should have air conditioning, and then 2.00, which is the luxury rate. I prefer the 1.60s for everyday use, not that there is a lot to choose between them. But I have the naive idea that a driver who has progressed to 1.60 must have a certain level of skill and experience. Also my random research study based on 'Cabs I have travelled in' suggests that the 1.60 drivers have slightly more English, and are certainly happy to use pidgin Chinese for a poor foreigner who speaks very little.

One feature of the taxis is that the drivers sit in a metal cage – the back of their seat is protected by a metal sheet, which then bends round and divides their seat from the front passenger seat. Up to the top of the seat level (or car window level) the metal is a solid sheet. Above seat level – i.e. car window height – it becomes metal bars. So money and receipts can be passed to and fro, but the driver is very well protected. Occasionally foreigners express surprise at this level of protection. If there is no crime in Beijing, why do taxi drivers need protecting? And well before the Olympics there will be taxi drivers 'volunteering' to drive in open cabs – or so we are told!

Returning to Beijing after almost two months away was less of a culture shock than I had expected – I seem to have slipped back into routine almost without noticing. But Beijing does seem much dirtier than I remembered – or maybe it is that I mind about the dirt more this time. And things that don't work. And the audiences at the theatre who talk, arrive late, push past you ignoring what is happening on stage, let their mobile phones ring. My flat itself is okay, a bit dreary and worn-looking compared to the open skies of Derbyshire countryside and hot clear days cycling in France, but fine for another year. Or at least it would be but they (the Beijing authorities?) have now demolished a lot of buildings around the block. For reasons best known to them the main work of removing the rubble is done at night, so the nights are noisy. And the dust and grit and dirt is intense. All my carpets, bedspread – and probably curtains but I haven't gone that far yet – have had to be washed, and the dirt that is rinsed out suggests they have all been to the beach for the day and rolled around in the sand.

The small corner shops have been torn down – not that I used them much but the owners were friendly and it gave a sense of community. They have been replaced by people selling things from tables – great for me as one of them sells phone cards, 100 RMB card for only 56, which means about thirty minutes international call for less than £5. I'm buying them in bulk as I fear the man will be moved on.

Demolition is rife in Beijing at present – all because of 2008. Modern shopping malls and apartment blocks are replacing the old courtyards and dilapidated offices and shops. Many of the foreigners are grief-stricken because Ya Bao Lu is being torn down – the old Russian market. It was a good place to buy clothes, silk, fur coats and so on, bargaining the prices down of course. I had never been there, but had heard about it. And it will be replaced by an all-American shopping mall. Sign of the times as Starbucks takes over. There are 65 KFCs (Kentucky Fried Chicken if you don't immediately recognise it; KFC is Beijing's favourite fast food I think) in Beijing and this week the first drive-thru was opened. This is such a novelty that apparently people are taking taxis rides just to have the experience of a drive-thru.

Since I returned I have noticed the number of new roads which are now complete in my part of Beijing: modern broad avenues, with street lighting, freshly tarmacked with road markings, pedestrian crossing lights and barriers along the middle separating the two highways. In one way I am delighted, because some serious roadworks which were on my bus route to work, and caused the bus to nearly tip over on occasion because the road was so uneven, are now finished. But the road that has appeared is about three lanes either way, modern, straight, fast – and I would guess a fair few cyclists will be killed by cars speeding along it. The development is so intense that one piece of road is completed, as soon as another is started. The new subway is also progressing – you can measure this by the progress made by the works above ground.

I shouldn't complain. If I were a Beijinger I would be delighted to be re-housed (and given compensation) in a modern apartment with an inside bathroom, running hot water, safe electrics and a play area. The journey time to work of an hour and more would be something to complain about, but many do not seem to mind, and somehow communities do seem to have been moved together. But living in a city which is one large building site (or feels like one) can be hard – and very noisy at night.

And now Teachers' Day. 10 September in China is Teachers' Day. The students come in with cards, flowers and chocolates, they read poems to their teachers, and wish you a happy year. Hard to know how much they mean it of course – but I am sure even the most cynical of us believes that this year these students really mean it.

We don't get the day off, but there are parties, and as I work at two schools I went to two parties. The first, at lunchtime, was with my colleagues from the vocational middle school. About a hundred of us all went to a large Western hotel near to the fourth ring road (Beijing actually now has a fifth ring road, so we were not that far out) where there were a further hundred retired teachers joining us. We were greeted by the head teacher, and ushered to tables. Drinks (soft drinks and beer) were served to us as we waited. There was a brief interlude for speeches, but most of the greetings and good wishes were lost in the noise. Why do I expect my students to be quiet when I am teaching them when the retired (and not yet retired) teachers simply talk through and over their boss trying to address them through a loudspeaker?

Speeches over, the 'leaders' – the head teacher and other senior members of the Education Authority – went from table to table 'toasting' the teachers, and the teachers went seriously into action getting food. It was just like a hoard of locusts; within minutes the dishes of food on the buffet were emptied: hot food, cold food, starters, main course, fruit and cream desserts, all disappeared on to plates and were taken back into the main dining room. Behind the scenes the staff must have wondered what had hit them. Answer: 200 teachers working in government schools. Impressive.

More food was brought; more food was eaten – and a fair bit was discarded – and then very abruptly (by Western standards) the event was over. Table upon table of guests just upped and left – some to resume retirement and others to go back to work. As the working teachers had had to start lessons early (7.35 a.m. instead of 8 a.m. in order to finish the morning early and get to the lunch) it seemed doubly unfair that they had to go back for afternoon classes – not my idea of celebrating a day, but still.

I was lucky and managed to have time for myself (including a much needed swim to have some exercise) before I went to the second do, with my other colleagues. This was an evening do, so it began at 5 p.m. The format was much the same, and again the retired teachers almost outnumbered those still working. There was much more alcohol available – in fact some were complaining that we needed more fruit juice, and this time it was very much a Chinese meal, with chopsticks (lunch had been a knife and fork affair – unusual for China), and *huge* amounts of food. No chance of running out here. This was a Chinese hotel where the staff knew what to expect. Shorter speeches, many more toasts, and an enormous amount of photographs. Someone was videoing it all and there were three or four other photographers. I just wonder what happens to all these photos. I never see them again, yet so many occasions are recorded in this way.

Again the event came to an abrupt ending by around 6.30. We upped and left (I was off to the theatre, an American ballet company), only to be brought up short as we reached the hotel entrance. It was pouring with rain. Most of us didn't have umbrellas, taxis were in short supply – and this was real, serious rain. Stair rods. So we stood and debated, watched others using their handbags as umbrellas, or a bag, or a book – but of course your feet and legs get soaked. Another Beijing speciality is loose paving stones – you step on one side, the slab tips and you spurt cold muddy water up the inside of your trousers, or up inside your skirt. And it's all self-inflicted because you stood on that paving stone. *So* annoying. Fortunately the theatre is close to the subway, so I walked with some teachers, sharing umbrellas, and didn't get too wet. And later the rain had eased, I found a taxi easily and got home to a cooler, fresher night. Teachers' Day over for this year (although a few staff were definitely worse for wear the next day – or even didn't show up at all).

One interesting sign of the times. One of my teacher colleagues, a woman in her mid/late thirties, has spent the summer holidays learning to drive. She is married, and has the one child, a daughter of twelve. Her husband is in the army, and lives in the barracks on the edge of Beijing. The teacher and her daughter live in a rented bungalow all week, to be close to her work and the daughter's school, and return home at weekends. I don't get the impression that they are extremely well off; more an ordinary family, which respects education, and certainly will spend to ensure the daughter succeeds. My colleague is paid by the hour, and does not want extra work as she likes to see her daughter off to school, and be there for her in the evening. She is a serious, slightly old-fashioned Chinese mother.

But now, she can drive and a car either has been, or shortly will be, bought. I don't think this would have happened a year ago. Then it was the young, well educated, single, or couples with no children, working for joint venture companies who were buying cars. Not people with careers in public service, putting their money into a child's education and future. But since China entered the WTO, taxes on imported cars have been slashed, and China's own car model is beginning to sell well. It doesn't bode well for Beijing's already over-crowded roads and the polluted air.

Enough for now. I have to get back to work after the interruption of Teachers' Day. After all we have to work for a further three weeks before the National Day holiday on 1 October and a week off. And I was reading that in England more and more people are putting in sixty-hour weeks as the norm!

Love to all from my relaxed China life, Sue

二〇〇二

Sometimes I have to remind myself why I came to China. I am not talking of the occasions when I feel homesick, it's too hot, or there's been a dust storm, the students are being difficult, or I've been in a taxi with a driver who keeps stopping to spit. No, I'm talking about the times when I'm feeling under-occupied, when I seem to be drifting in a very relaxed (even bored) approach to work, and only need to put in half a working day by Western standards to be regarded as extremely conscientious and diligent. I have worked for so long in England that to have free evenings, to have time to shop – or even swim – in the middle of the day, to see friends for lunch, to go to an art exhibition on a weekday, all such activities make me feel guilty and I start to question whether I am earning my salary.

Then I remind myself of why I came to China. One of the main reasons was to get away from the long hours culture where work intrudes into evenings and weekends, where email rules and you are never more than a (mobile) phone call away from the office. I came to have time to pause, to reflect, to learn a new language, to cope with a very different culture, and to have time to question and make discoveries.

To say I am enjoying this is an understatement. Most of the time (there are always the off-days in any job) it is a privilege to work as a teacher and as a manager without excessive pressure. To have time not only to prepare classes, but also to reflect on them afterwards and to think of improvements. My colleagues are teachers of English who are desperate to learn, to improve their own pronunciation, to widen and modernise their vocabulary. It is daunting to be seen as omniscient about English particularly when I am well aware of my own shortcomings, of the rapid change in language, and how different English-English is from American-English or Australian-English. What is correct depends on your location – and many native speakers here are also aware of the rapidly developing Chinese-English, Chinglish.

If you question whether work can be a privilege, the answer is yes, it can, when part of your job description is 'To bring respect into education, respect between students, respect between teachers, respect for students, respect for teachers'. There is even an Association for the Development of Respect in Education, set up by a former Chinese head teacher who visited Sweden and whose ideas were changed by seeing the teaching methods there. Idealistic maybe, but surely there should be room for some idealism in education?

Being a foreigner here adds a unique de-stressing factor into my working life. For large parts of my working day I have to communicate through an interpreter. This means I have to carefully consider what I want to say, keep it brief and to the point. Then I have a pause, while my comments are translated, there is a reply and that is then translated back to me. It sounds cumbersome, and can be slow – but it is also excellent discipline and forces you to think before you speak. I miss being able to react immediately. I miss, as a manager, being able to intervene fast in a difficult situation. But time and again, even if the immediate crisis has to be handled by others, the long-term remedy can be put in place once the immediate crisis is over, and actually maybe a better remedy because there has to be time for reflection and then explanation.

For example, we had a rash of truancy. Some students disappeared completely, and others just hid on the school premises (in a store cupboard, in the toilets etc.). On investigation it became clear that the teachers didn't even bother to report truanting, as they felt no action would be taken. Nor had they paused to think that maybe something was less than attractive about their teaching if students preferred to spend four hours of a hot day in the toilets (these are Chinese toilets, remember) than in their classroom. So we have had to improve the reporting and monitoring system – and also had to look at our teaching methods. Working through a translator has ensured I dealt with this with a certain amount of tact and diplomacy, rather than attempting an instant fix.

Outside of the working day my life has been considerably enriched and enhanced by transferring to another culture. In many ways my standard of living has dropped – no car, a very small and rather old flat, running hot water only in the bathroom, two rings for cooking, limited television and radio and so on. But my quality of life is amazing. I am in one of the most interesting cities in the world; in a single month I have seen the RSC, Spanish and Russian ballet, French films and a Giacometti sculpture exhibition. This is where free evenings really do mean something!

Lifelong learning has become a reality as I gradually see my level of Chinese increasing, while around me everyone – from taxi driver to teacher, policeman to politician – is learning English. I mix with people of so many nationalities and backgrounds that there is no longer a norm. My understanding of global politics is vastly changed now I see a world with China as the centre. I have become very aware of my ignorance about the history, geography and politics of Australia and New Zealand, yet these are other Commonwealth countries so when I celebrated the Queen's Jubilee at the British Embassy it was with Australians, New Zealanders and Canadians (not Americans). I miss Europe and European culture, and find an hour spent at the French Lycée has me dreaming of time in France, the cultural identity is so strong and distinct.

Not that these reflections completely stifle my guilt – not when I consider my students. Not only are their days long, leaving home before 6 a.m. and not getting home until after 5 p.m., followed by hours of homework, but many also attend extra classes at weekends. The school year is divided into two very long terms, one from September until mid-January with only a week off in early October to celebrate the National Holiday, and the second runs from mid-February, after the month-long Spring Festival holiday, until mid-July with only one week off for the May Day holiday. Nearly five months of unbroken schooling, ending with two months of hot muggy temperatures, and those life-deciding end-of-year examinations. Never again will I regard air conditioning as a luxury after battling to keep myself and thirty students awake for two periods after lunch.

2002 Continued…

二
〇
〇
二

Dear All,

Well, the National Congress has come and gone; Jiang Zemin is no longer General Secretary of the Party – but, really, nothing has changed. He still dominates the news coverage, his successor is known as quiet and is living up to that. While it was happening in Beijing the Congress certainly did make its presence felt, and I did get a bit caught up in the hype of 'setting the agenda for the twenty-first century'. Partly this was just the strangeness of it all – each morning the blackboard at the school gate had information about the Congress (handwritten, beautifully, in coloured chalk – very reminiscent of the fifties and primary school in Suffolk). I am not used to political events being reported quite that locally. Also it is hard to live here with the constant construction, the almost perceptible increase in traffic daily as private car ownership explodes (blocking the roads with new cars being badly driven by inexperienced drivers), the drive to learn English, the desire to move forward and change, without thinking that the twenty-first century will be China's century. So some of the *China Daily* political reportage seems to be true.

The Congress did bring one special joy – the heating in Beijing was turned on a fortnight early. It is hard to imagine how odd life is when the heating (or lack of it) is centrally controlled. When I came back to Beijing in late October I was immediately taken aback by the cold. It was below freezing at night; there was a stiff breeze, my flat windows are by no means snugly fitting – it was cold. The two schools where I work were even worse. Open corridors, cold, cold classrooms – and absolutely no sources of heat. At least in the flat, cooking, or even candles, gave off some warmth. Also the IKEA nightlights pour out heat and can make my room pleasantly warm. In the schools there was nothing. In the flat I could get into bed (jet lag meant that was a good option) and there was warmth seeping from other flats around too – at school all we could do was sit in coats and gloves. My teaching became extremely interactive – and just plain active. After twenty minutes I would get the students to stand up, run round the room, jog on the spot, anything to get the circulation going. I wrote copiously on the blackboard, and the coldest student got the pleasure of cleaning it off, with massive energy.

The heating was not due until November 15; until then everyone was making do with electric heated oil-filled radiators (the lift even has one); or – favourite trick but so expensive and inefficient – air conditioners reversed, so instead of cooling the warm air they heated the cold air. Needless to say the city was plagued with power cuts. Another rather more than trivial annoyance to those of us Westerners who have fine wispy hair is that the effect of hot air-conditioned air was to turn this fine wispy hair into *very dry* fine wispy hair. Chinese hair is thicker, and better behaved. I was walking static. I even gave a taxi driver an electric shock one day when I passed him money. The metal security strip (put in all the notes to prevent forgery) must have picked it up. Mind you, the air conditioner I have in my flat does not do the reversing trick.

Just as I was beginning to recover from jet lag and not wanting to spend evenings asleep under a thick duvet and two blankets, I picked up the rumour that the heating was coming on two weeks early. Of course that may just be kindness, but I reckon it was the National Congress starting on 9 November that really swung it. Hotels, public buildings, restaurants, all needed heating. And wonderfully, on 31 October, heating came on. Then I discovered another bit of China folklore. My heating – I think – is covered by my rent. But many Chinese do not pay the heating part of the rent until they absolutely have to. So I was wandering around lightly clad (i.e. one tee-shirt, one sweater, rather than thermals, two long-sleeved tee-shirts, a shirt and then a thick sweater *à la* Chinese), nattering about having heat and my colleagues were denying the heating was on, or then grinning and saying, 'Oh, maybe I haven't paid for the heating.'

Typically, of course, then the sun came out, the weather got warmer, we ceased to have night frosts and the wind dropped. The weather is as perverse in China as in England. It hasn't lasted; now the frost is regular and shaded areas do not thaw by day. But it is bearable now – at last – the fabric of buildings has got warm.

We can actually work normally in class. And one of the joys of Beijing is that it is dry, so I see the sun most days. It makes a huge difference. I am still woken by the sun every morning, and come back to a flat which feels warm partly because sunshine has warmed it through the morning. My washing gets dry on the balcony – if it didn't it would freeze overnight as the balcony glass leaves a lot to be desired (but we are not risking replacing the cracked and broken glass for fear that the whole frame will go. Better glass covering 95% of the area rather than no glass at all). I have heavy curtains separating balcony cold air from the main room of the flat.

I was back in England in October partly because it was National Holiday here so no work for a week, and then two of my Chinese colleagues came to visit the university. I get the best of the National Holiday – I see all the decorations, the lights, the flowers, the tidying of the city to celebrate the fifty-third anniversary of the People's Republic. This year grander than ever, because with an eye to thrift and economy, the decorations were to 'make do' (with some additions) for the National Congress a month later. Of course for the Congress, national flags were added – from every shop doorway, block of flats, lampposts, trees – you name it, there was a flag. And more lights.

The Chinese had an interesting time while in England. They longed for Chinese food – but when we went to the local Chinese restaurant (recommended as the most authentic by Chinese students) they were disappointed, both by the food, and that the staff did not speak Chinese (apart from one waiter who is a university student from mainland China). They went shopping, and were confused to the point of being distressed that Derby does not have taxis cruising around to be hailed in the street. Taxi ranks do exist in Beijing, but you hardly need to use them. Also pedestrianisation and very restricted parking was confusing (not to mention the lack of a *driver*). The idea that I drove them, we parked, we walked to a restaurant, and then I drove them back, was very strange. Just as strange as it is to us that the head of a medium-sized school has a driver and a lovely luxury Audi, and the school has two other cars and drivers, to be used when required. My guess is that the young Chinese do not have such a problem adapting; my colleagues were males over fifty, not used to doing much for themselves, and certainly not used to adjusting, being flexible, or having various requests refused. Of course the Chinese way is to say, 'Yes' to the request and not to actually do it. We had a real clash of cultures when they wanted to see into a student room in a hall of residence and I attempted to explain that this was the student's private place and we needed permission of the student. Back came, 'The head teacher would like to see inside the room.' When they eventually realised this was not possible, they set off across the grass border next to the building with the aim of looking in through a window and taking photos! I managed to resolve this, but I think they still are not clear why there was a problem.

On the work front, one of the two schools where I work is still a real struggle. The links I have made with France are put on hold while the powers that be investigate the possibility of links in Canada; they risk losing all links with the delays (and are losing students as parents move their children to other schools as they lose confidence here because of the delays). The school is due to have an inspection in a couple of weeks; on all the criteria it fails, and will be closed (numbers, facilities, qualifications of teachers etc.) but I gather it will be fine, due to influence.

We have had a visit for two weeks of eleven students from Nuremberg, Germany. This was fun; the two teachers with them spoke reasonable English, and on occasion I played tour guide, showing off my adopted city. (Yes, they hit the cold patch. A hotel with no heating; they borrowed bedding and clothes to see them through. I didn't dare tell them the heating came on two days after they left.)

The students were impressive too. They were living with their Chinese partners, so finding out the reality of Chinese life. Most were in reasonable housing; only one was in a house with no bathroom or toilet – and that was only because the Chinese boy comes from an army family. A foreign visitor is not allowed to live on the army base, so they had to stay in a house not normally used. Nevertheless they had to eat what was offered, and cope with living alongside a family where the one child spoke (some) German, and they spoke no Chinese. They managed.

It was interesting for me to be reminded of the maturity of Western teenagers. There is the clear difference in sophistication – make-up, clothes, material belongings – but also such a difference in attitude. German sixteen-year-olds manage their own money; when put into groups to do some work, they get on with it, quietly. Chinese seventeen-year-olds, or eighteen or nineteen-year-olds, do not have any idea about money, still wear the clothes that their parents choose, of course do not wear make-up and few of them have travelled. And put Chinese teenagers into groups to work, and all you get is noise, noise, noise, until they get used to the idea of freedom and being responsible.

Of course German students go to school from 8 a.m.–1 p.m., or maybe 3 p.m. Chinese students get to school at 7.30 a.m. (and travelling in Beijing means they leave home by 6.30), don't get home until seven each evening, and then have a lot of homework. As one German girl said, 'The Chinese homes are where they eat, work and sleep; our homes are where we live.'

At the other school, life is good. I can see how my ideas are paying off and changing things. I do have students who – most of the time – are mature. Their level of English is improving rapidly. About half of the group of thirty-four will have no problem in coming to England to study. They write well, and can speak fluently. About another ten can certainly manage a foundation year and then a degree. For all of them, money, the fear of the unknown, parents' fear of terrorism, and a belief that they won't get visas means they still have not completely committed themselves to study abroad, but most of them will. I have now had a one-to-one interview with all thirty-four of them, and begin to find out more about them: one girl whose mother died when she was seven, who now lives with her grandparents because her father has remarried; an eighteen-year-old boy whose father has left home and they don't know where he is (this is a cause of deep shame in China still) – and other tales of unhappiness. They have also been writing about China in the last fifty years – the Cultural Revolution then becomes personal – and about their own lives. So girls write about how they are of less worth because their grandparents wanted a boy; or if they do study abroad, which will cost their parents so much, then they must repay their parents in the future.

STOP PRESS: I am listening to CCTV 9 news in English, and they have just reported on a demonstration by members of Amnesty International in New York. A protest to coincide with World Children's Day, something which is big in China, and Amnesty is definitely being approved of in the broadcast!

Back to my students. I have brought in two serious innovations. The first is English Corner (i.e. informal talk in English as a form of self-help to learn more, widely practised in China). My innovation is that I have Grade 3 students running it, each leading a group of six younger students. The students are unsupervised in a classroom over lunchtime. This is almost unheard of. It is working; they are well behaved, seem to work and appreciate it, and maybe some English is learnt. The Chinese teachers just say it is because the best students have been selected – but even if this is the case, it is working!

The other innovation – and now you will see quite how groundbreaking all this is – is that I now have students borrowing books and taking them home. Not from the school library, of course (you thought a library was for borrowing books? No, it is for *storing* books. Books cannot be borrowed as they might get damaged). Instead we have bought some books – modern, short, easy to read, with coloured covers, up to date – such as *Love Story* – remember the film? – and the Grade 3 students can borrow them. They sign them out – we have two library monitors – and then bring them back. I actually don't think this is happening. They tell me it is, but so far all I have seen is the students sitting, supervised, in rows in their classroom at lunchtime, reading the books. But at least they are reading, and the books are easier than *Gulliver's Travels*, *Robinson Crusoe*, Dickens, Thackeray or the Brontës.

Must go; work tomorrow starts at the crack as always. Will I ever get used to getting up before 6.30 a.m., being on the bus by 7.15 and starting teaching or meetings at 8?

Love to all, Sue

2003

二
〇
〇
三

Dear Everyone,

A quick update from sunny – but cold – Beijing, before I fly to the frozen north to do examining for the British Council. Temperatures here in Beijing are reported as 5 to minus 3 at present (centigrade, no Fahrenheit here). It has been, supposedly, minus 3 to minus 10, but I don't believe that because you see water running rather than frozen, and my hands and nose don't freeze the second I put them outside. Also, thinking about it, I don't get ice on the inside of the balcony windows, and I am sure I would if it was really freezing out. I guess the quoted temperatures are ground temperatures, in the shade. But we have long sunny days, blue skies, and there is already a sense of spring. And yes, the days are lengthening; when I came back after Christmas it was dark around 4.30 p.m., and even now that is delayed until 5 or 5.15 p.m.

But where I am going later today, Shenyang, northeast China (north of North Korea), not that far from the Russian border, it will be cold. Temperatures of minus 3 to minus 10, and the windows of the minibus we travel in will freeze up on the inside, even packed with expat examiners. So it is heavy boots, a warm wool suit, and a heavy waterproof jacket. The suit is wonderful – I have had my one and only Jaeger suit (bought five years ago at factory prices in Belper) copied. So my Jaeger cut-price £50 suit is now reproduced in equally high quality fabric, made to measure and cost all of £40! I think there is a discount as my tailor is delighted to have a Jaeger copy. Mysteriously my original suit is being 'dry cleaned' at the tailor's expense, so I have my new suit but not the original yet – I get that back next week. Is it being copied by the tailor's friends and relations?

Life at the tailor's is one of the joys here. I am very much one of their favoured clients (mainly because I am not seen as the typical client; I tend to be thrilled with my purchases, whereas most ambassadors' wives and their Russian customers are much pickier). They like the difference – I am tall, not skinny, and clearly don't have Chinese colouring, so we can try different colours from the ones they use for their Chinese customers. They also are impressed that I work in Chinese government schools, teaching children who could be related to them. But best of all, I give them English lessons. 'May I help you *please*', 'That looks *beautiful*', 'Would you like to try ano*th*er colour?', and 'Yell*ow*, gree*en*, re*d*, w*ooo*l', are phrases that echo around their booth, while I sit on a stool and am fed satsumas. I think we are going to formalise this a bit more after the Chinese New Year holiday. I will get clothes for free (or just the cost of the material) and they will have regular 'bespoke' (or should it be tailor-made – sorry) English lessons.

The shop's owner, Amy, from Shanghai, is away at present, getting married. This causes hoots of laughter among the rest of the female staff. 'Amy not here,' they say, point at their wedding fingers indicating a ring, prance up and down mimicking a bride, and then laugh. I think the laughter is mainly to do with the lot of Chinese wives; she thinks she is having a great romantic occasion, but they know better. Soon she will have a husband to look after back here in Beijing (so no family to fall back on), shopping, cooking, cleaning – as well as working. And then the obligatory one child – preferably a son, who will be cared for, spoilt, cosseted from morning to night. As one of them explained, in very fractured English, she has no time to be married as she spends all her time looking after her child. Certainly close relationships between couples are not obvious; the Chinese anyway are not demonstrative in public, although this is changing; the teenagers are like teenagers everywhere, certainly in Beijing. You also see elderly couples holding hands – even President Jiang Zemin is seen holding hands, or patting the arm of his wife. But the demands of working lives and the incredibly long hours mean couples are not together that much and sex is still regarded as risky, particularly by the women, because of the single-child policy. Access to birth-control is easy, but also abortion is widespread because if a second child is conceived, it must be aborted. So women, naturally, retain the fear of pregnancy once they have the first child.

By contrast with the Chinese, my working life for the past few weeks has been quite pleasant. The teachers seem to be working about sixteen-hour days, with exams, exam marking and then meetings which go on until late at night. So much has to be done before the spring holiday. Precisely what happens in these meetings is unclear; decisions are not made, or if made one day, they are reversed the next. A fair bit is the reading out of policy statements from the Education Commission (the district, or the city, or national), then interpretation of these policies. I gather that this year there will be more university places in Chinese universities (1.7 million going to university) but to allow time for the marking of the entrance examinations, they are bringing the exams forward by a month. Just think of that – if it was announced in England around February that A-levels and GCSEs would be taken a month earlier, could we cope?

Another aspect of a teacher's life here is the extra work they do, with the additional classes being organised, both for their own students (to try to ensure good exam marks) and for external customers. My school keeps getting new brass plaques to put up at the gate: 'Beijing Centre for English Examinations' (except it will be spelt *Center*); 'Beijing Centre for Computer Examinations' – and so on. I am not sure if the teachers get paid any extra for running classes for these examination candidates; I rather doubt it. Certainly the young teachers I have been training just have to do this as part of their main job. Twenty to thirty hours' teaching a week, and then a further twelve over the weekend, so they only get a morning or an afternoon off.

The Languages College, my other place of work, is going through a very difficult time. There seem to be about four people in charge. While I am around as part of the senior management team, it seems I both act as a restraint – foreigner present so don't argue – and also I tend to (unwittingly) ask questions pushing towards a decision, or assume a decision has been taken and therefore we are working to that, so we can move on. What I was not aware of is that once I am not there they go round all the decisions again, reverse them, then re-adopt them – and then discover that the latest policy change does not allow for this anyway.

A good example of all this has been the plans to send the French students abroad once they finish high school here. I had made links with Toulouse University last summer; an agreement was finalised, but never signed by the Chinese, and then gradually everything was quietly dropped. Plans to link to the Lycée, to bring in teachers from Alliance Française, to get students slightly involved with the French community here in Beijing, using the library, going to films etc., were all shelved. Then I learnt that the plan now being pursued was to send the students to French-speaking Canada, and this was being encouraged by the Education Commission. A delegation was coming over from Quebec, and new deals would be struck.

This did eventually happen (by late November), but although contracts were signed, the Canadians returned home and nothing more happened. Then (all of this inside information coming from my assistant, Joanna, of course) there were numerous meetings among the Chinese staff here, going on until late into the night so they could connect to Canadian working time (I think Canada is about twelve to thirteen hours behind China, so you can imagine the delay). Faxes were sent, and the whole meeting sat by the fax machine, hoping for a reply. None came.

Then another of the senior managers introduced an agent from France, with links into private colleges there – but it then became apparent that the students would not be able to go to state universities in France, but would have to pay. The attraction of France is that once in the state system, education is free for all students, whether French or overseas.

So now it is back to trying to revive the Toulouse link (which of course has meant I have been phoning and emailing to France, urgently, late into the evening, but at least I do that from the comfort of my flat). It seems it will work, but now that the spring holiday is about to begin, nothing more can be done until mid-February.

Incidentally, one lovely tale about the Canadian delegation. There is now a suspicion that they were not really serious (because of the lack of follow-up) and the Chinese are angry with themselves for not spotting this. Because the Canadians brought their wives with them (first indication they were not serious), and then, when they went off on a sightseeing trip to Xi'an for three days, they paid to keep their hotel rooms here in Beijing. This is gross extravagance to the Chinese. Already it had been remarked upon that they were staying in luxury Western hotels, but then to retain the rooms for three days when they were not using them – this was clear evidence of frivolous tourism rather than serious educational bridge-building.

Before you think I am too critical of life here, I should add that I am sure it is the same everywhere – and you have to admire the way the Chinese are trying to change, to move forward, and to improve the standard of living. The sheer energy being poured out is amazing. My block of flats is now surrounded by construction work, most of it being done at night – new apartments, shopping malls, and an overground light railway. The working conditions are awful – a building site seems unattractive to me at the best of times, but at night, with floodlighting, freezing temperatures and sometimes really high winds? I think the night working is partly to reduce disruption by day to the neighbours, but also is due to a rule they have here about lorry traffic. Heavy lorries, cement-mixers and the like are simply not allowed into the city centre by day because of the traffic implications. They can only move around at night, with permission. So if the site needs deliveries of cement, steel girders, or pre-fab walls, all of it happens at night. Regarding traffic, not a bad idea!

The impact of all this construction has had the effect of lowering residential rents. I have met two new arrivals from England recently, who are flat hunting. They do not want a Chinese apartment like mine, but seem able to rent a much more modern, Western apartment in a compound for prices which are less than a £100 a month more than I pay. A year ago the difference would have been twice that. This is partly due to market forces – more flats are available – and also to a change in policy – foreigners can now live in previously designated Chinese areas, without special permission. So the inflated prices for foreigners in specific areas have gone.

Traffic, on the other hand, gets worse, and will continue to do so until some of the new undergrounds and light railways are up and running (two to three years away). Meanwhile more and more private cars are being bought and used. Even worse, more and more Chinese (particularly men) are learning to drive and getting licences. They cannot afford to buy cars, but can afford to rent, at least once a year. So now, with the actual Chinese New Year still a fortnight away (1 February), and most people only getting the week off at that time (it is only teachers who get the month), there are no cars available to rent over the actual day; they have all been booked in advance. Just think, the roads will be filled with inexperienced drivers, stressed out with the family reunion (England at Christmas time) in rented cars. A good time not to be here. Trains, buses, flights, hotels – all are booked out; extra flights are being laid on and 'special' flights direct from the mainland to Taiwan (one way only) are being arranged for the holiday period. (Normally you cannot fly direct PRC/Taiwan – I gather the flights are for Taiwanese people to go home for the holiday, but the arrangement is not permanent, and will only be China – Taiwan, not Taiwan – China; planes will do that leg of the journey with only the crew on board.)

On a personal level I am just beginning to think about the implication of only having a few months left. One more term. It's good – the students at the vocational school who want to go to university in England have shown they can get to the necessary level of English. Twenty out of thirty-four have completed application forms, and a few more would have done, but the threat of a war is meaning grandparents are saying they cannot go. It is too far away, and in matters like this the elderly are respected. But with that project complete, and a team in place to carry on with the curriculum we have developed, there is actually less to do apart from teaching out the term. At the Languages College I will have the French link to establish – unless it changes again. I won't mind not going through another winter in Beijing. Most of the time it is okay – it is dry (too dry), sunny, and clear – but when it is clouded and polluted, it is awful. I have had a cold, which is almost unshiftable because even if the cold gets better, the muck and pollution have the same effect.

I can also see, now that I am well into the second year here, the amount of change and development going on around me. I have been lucky; I have caught, just about, some of the old Beijing. Soon there will definitely be more cars than bicycles (and bicycles are now confined to cycle lanes on main roads); the low-level courtyard housing in the hutongs is disappearing, replaced by flats. The foreigners complain at this, but I am sure for those living in them, a modern flat is preferable (would there have been an outcry at destroying the back to back houses in England?), with an inside bathroom, running water, no need to share, no damp (well, not as much damp. I am not convinced that some of the new blocks are high quality buildings). There are more and more shopping malls and fewer small – and not so small – corner-type shops.

People arriving now will have less adjustment to make; they can easily buy Western food – is it only eighteen months since I had to search for coffee, and even fresh milk? Now I can buy a huge variety of cheeses – I've even discovered one which is flavoured with mustard grains, just as I buy in England. Dragon Seal wines have just produced a new Vin Nouveaux, in collaboration with a French company.

Well, I guess I have a plane to catch, so should stop. Shenyang is not so developed as Beijing, but I will be ensconced in the luxury of a four-star hotel – well protected from the cold. The lack of development is evident; people still stare at foreigners in the street – and the standard of English of the students we are testing will be noticeably lower than in Beijing. It is also a hive of political activity, because it is so close to North Korea. Americans fly in and out (there is an American consulate in Shenyang) – and there are large delegations in Beijing as well. It is certainly interesting seeing the world and its politics and power play from the other side – as much as one can believe any of the news (either here or off the internet – oh, that's another change I've seen; I now can get BBC on the internet all the time. A year ago it was impossible, then it was sporadic; now it seems to be permanent).

So good wishes to everyone for the Year of the Sheep (or Goat – the two seem interchangeable here). It is not a good year for a baby to be born (apparently if you are born in the Year of the Sheep you will have a difficult and unhappy life). So pregnant women are queuing to be induced at various private maternity hospitals. But, as my cynical assistant, Joanna, points out, 'Any child born in the Year of the Sheep will get to a key school and to university; there will be very little competition.' She, however, is biased; her younger sister is a Sheep, and Joanna reckons her younger sister has had a far easier life than she herself has had (because, of course, as the elder sister, Joanna broke down all the barriers, and also came to Beijing first, on her own. Her younger sister has just had to follow that path).

Love, Sue

Hi,

Not a precise date because by the time some of you get this not only will it be early April, but I will be back in England. Yes – a big change (well, not really, I am due to finish here in a few months, but it is being brought forward). So I will email this, but the hard copy version will be sent by UK snail mail once I am back and when I have got my computer sorted and printer in place.

So what is happening? Well, a lot really. First of all, back in England over the spring holiday, I agreed redundancy with the university. So I will need to get back, and begin to sort my CV and think what I am going to do next. That will be easier from England (even though I know I can get all the newspapers and the vacancies by the internet). But a lot of other things are driving my decision to return to England before the end of this term – first of all, SARS. No one is really too sure about this outbreak/epidemic at present. There is a lot of talk and gossip – and a lot of concern. It seems to be mainly affecting southern China – but no one really knows (nor is anyone sure how much we should believe the government information). For the first time my registration at the British Embassy seems to be useful – I automatically get the weekly bulletin on information. No reason to go back to the UK, but there are one or two areas we are advised not to travel to.

Friends intending to come to China on holiday tours – Beijing/Shanghai/Xi'an for the Terracotta Warriors, the Three Gorges – are emailing to ask if I have any information. One or two of the IELTS examiners seem anxious, and no one really feels totally clear about the true situation. There are a lot of 'jokes' about people in lifts in Hong Kong, but no one really laughs. We are told that SARS affects people over fifty more seriously than the youngsters – but some of us are over fifty so that is not very consoling!

But there are other anxieties too – what is happening about the situation in Iraq? Not only are students concerned about coming to England, but I can tell my bosses are a bit uneasy about my being so far from home (as they see it).

There is also a lot of anxiety here about the students getting their visas. I took the university applications back to England with me when I went back for the holiday, and brought offer letters back. Next money has to be sent over as deposits to secure places in the halls of residence, and the students have to apply for visas from the Embassy. We seem to have sorted out a way for the money to be sent from one bank in China to the university bank in England, but the head teacher here is keen that I go back to England to ensure that the visas are approved. The decision will actually be made in Beijing, and I am relatively confident that the students will have no problem. They can apply as a group. There is no such thing as a 'group visa', but they can be considered as a group, and given the preparation that we have done, and the records at the Embassy (this is known as a recognised programme), I think it should be fine. But the head is right – if there are problems, then at least if I am in England I can get the university to assist in sorting out the visas.

Sorry – some of this is a bit boring if you are not involved in getting students into England, but the writing about is therapeutic. I *am* worried about the visas, how do I know they will get them? You always hear the bad news stories. But at least everything is on the way and we have a lot of time.

So, when I got back here after spending the Chinese New Year holiday in England (everywhere so green, Radio 4, newspapers readily available, shops where I can just buy what I want and it is not an adventure), I had a meeting with the head. Partly I needed to sort out job-hunting in England (not a lot of use trying to find jobs in education if you are not back until the summer holidays have started). It all went much more smoothly than I expected – and the outcome is that I will return in a week or so (flights to be sorted) – and the school has given me a new contract! I will return to China twice a year, in October and May, for a stint of intensive teaching. And the contract runs until May 2005. How's that for long-term planning?

Of course, the real reason it all went so easily is purely pragmatic. A teacher is coming over from Singapore (the school has a link into Singapore) and no accommodation has been arranged. Like so much here it has been left to the last minute. If I return home, then my flat is free, complete with furniture and rent paid up – so the Singaporean teacher can move in. Not sure how someone from a country which doesn't tolerate chewing gum on the streets will feel about the general grubbiness of this area. But that's not my problem. And it makes it all much easier for me.

The plan is that I will come back after the May holiday, once the visas are confirmed, and all the paperwork of cash, receipts, etc. are sorted, and do some final teaching and the end-of-term exams. I will also do more work with the current Grade 2s, just before they become the final year students in September. The money the school will save on my salary will be diverted to employ some expat part-time teachers who will keep on teaching the students who are due to come to England in September, and work with the group who will come in September 2004 – and so on.

I'm suddenly feeling a bit torn. Of course, I'm pleased I am not needed here as it shows I have taught them well, but at the same time it is all moving very fast. I keep reminding myself that this is a success – but at the same time I feel a huge sense of sadness at leaving. And of course, England is something of an unknown. At the moment, the only work I have for the future is a promise of some IELTS examining back in England.

So – what will I miss about China? The excitement, the buzz, the sense that I have achieved something – that every day is a new adventure. In England it is such a conversation stopper (or maybe starter) to say 'Oh, I work in China' – and it gets you out of awkward situations (like why don't I go to the dentist regularly). Being one of the redundant over-50s doesn't have quite the same ring. And of course there is just the sadness/anti-climax of something like this coming to an end. I talked about it for so long, then I did it; the first group of students will be going to England (and a few to France), so the job is done. What next?

One thing I will miss is the truly cosmopolitan nature of my life here. Beijing is not only (of course) full of Chinese, but my closest friends include Americans, Australians, Greek-Australians,

Chileans. And so many have stories to tell – they have worked in so many different places, have had such a range of experiences, so many are people who decided to take the challenge, to take 'the road less travelled by'. They seem to live less burdened lives – no home, no mortgage, no ties. Yet they are not 'drop outs'. They are doing serious work, not that well paid for the most part, but they are well off by Chinese standards. Maybe that is part of the attraction.

I have to stop – not only is it too sad to think about what – and who – I am leaving behind. But also I have to get packed, give away plants, arrange to leave some of my belongings here (no time to get them sorted for safe transport home), and as I am coming back before too long, then I can do a second trip carrying stuff then. Fortunately, friends here want some of my furnishings (not to mention my toaster, vases, IKEA lamp, a couple of rugs, the carpet, computer and desk chair). I promise myself a trip to IKEA once I am back in England, and then I can buy one or two items which I have had here, and I'll feel slightly less homesick for my Beijing flat.

So now I am in the midst of a whirl of evenings out, plus finalising the teaching, setting out a lesson plan for the next part of the term. Once that is done, I will feel able to relax a bit, and focus on the next step. Fortunately I do have my barn back in England, so even though there are still tenants in my house, I do have a space I can move back into. Better still, I did manage to get the phone line working finally over the holiday, so I will be able to plug in the computer and get online again. And I have a new desk, put together from a complicated flat pack. It's huge, including a drawer, a keyboard shelf which rolls in and out under the desk surface, a shelf on the side for the hard drive – I am so impressed by my prowess at assembling furniture. One thing China has made me is more self sufficient, more prepared to have a go. I am less concerned about doing things 'the right way' and instead just get on and do it. I also seem – at the moment at least – less worried about work than I expected. China has made me feel that everything is possible, that something will turn up. Surely if I could make it work in Beijing, it will be okay back in England? Of course that ignores the support of having paid employment and a relatively high salary. But redundancy seems less daunting than I would have expected. Who knows how long this positive mood will last, but I'll cling to it while I can. And the fact that I will be coming back, that the 'awfully big adventure' is not over, certainly softens the blow.

So, see you all soon.

Love, Sue

Dear Everyone,

Yes, I am back in Beijing – a strangely subdued post-SARS Beijing, but still Beijing, and much as I remember. I am only here for a couple of weeks, to do some teaching, to help with the next group of students who will go to England in September 2004, to see friends and collect the rest of my belongings. You'll remember I was planning to return here in May, but the SARS outbreak put a stop to that, so my luggage has been sitting waiting for me to come and pick it up for about six months. Of course a lot of the clothes I left here were summer clothes (thinking I need them in May; I'll probably just ditch them now!). And I find myself with a free Saturday afternoon, and a computer to hand, so I decided to send a quick letter (well, a rather long email, but it is either that or postcards, and I'll be back before they arrive).

The first thing I notice about Beijing is that it is less of a hubbub than I remember. Tourist places, Wang Fu Jing Street for example, are not crammed full of bodies. Shops seem quieter, and in some areas there are clearly less 'foreigners'. When I point this out to friends here, they agree, although for those who stayed throughout the summer their first thought is that life is back to normal. Of course, it is nothing like the deserted Beijing at the peak of the SARS but it is quieter, more like a Western capital city rather than the 'teeming millions' of Asia. I am sure it will revert to its former intensity, but it is interesting to be here before the whole SARS episode is over.

I find it hard to really comprehend the scope of the whole SARS outbreak. Imagine a city where all the schools are closed, where people don't go out, where most companies close down, where the universities are closed. The best I can do is to imagine the week of Christmas to the New Year, when we all have a patch of 'limbo time', being extended. There is a similarity – at Christmas most of the shops (still) close, so we all tend to be at home, and feel cooped up. But with SARS it went on for months. No one talks very much about it. I learn that Western hotels and apartment blocks were virtually deserted, often inhabited by just one or two stalwarts. People I meet who experienced this, living almost completely alone (isolated business men for example) seem to have become slightly mad; they still suck up contact with outsiders as if craving the drug of company. The Chinese say little; I am just left with this sense of a long patch of virtual hibernation, with people going out close to home, for shopping, for exercise, for diversion – and living a lot on email, internet, DVDs, and phone calls. I think for some it was a time of getting to know your neighbours. Beijing is a *huge* city, with so many having to travel for at least an hour to get to work in the centre. Just like us, life revolves around work and family, and local communities are not as strong as they once were – particularly for those who have been 're-housed' in the suburbs, maybe with people they do not know. (There has been a programme of this – demolishing decaying city centre blocks and building much nicer, larger lower level apartments, surrounded by green spaces.) The SARS period allowed people – forced people? – to meet their neighbours.

It is also almost impossible to grasp the implications of schools having been closed from May onwards. Everything seems to be going as normal, so does that mean no education from May to July makes no difference and by October the pupils have all caught up, and everything is normal? What does that say about the need to attend school? Of course no one is actually going to answer a question from me, because it sounds so critical. But I am curious. How did the children catch up? Did they have additional classes at home? Has the school been putting on extra classes? (I'm not sure how they would be fitted in, although I have found out that there are some extra classes at the weekend.)

I did ask one young Chinese woman who has been at university about the impact of SARS. She was due to graduate in the summer, and had all her final exams. So I asked her what had happened, and she told me that they had not had exams. 'The dean said health is more important than exams,' was the way she put it. So she seems to have graduated, to have been given all her certificates and is now working on the basis of these qualifications, but actually did not do end-of-year exams.

By contrast, the university entrance exams did take place – but in very specialised conditions. Students had their temperature taken (that seems to be the best early indicator of SARS) and were either well spread out in large exam halls, or some took the exams in isolation. Again I am puzzled as to how they prepared for these high pressure exams – private tutoring? Small classes? Work on the internet? I don't know. But life is very much back to normal, students have progressed, and SARS is hardly mentioned.

It does seem that the teachers got paid. I think all the people working in state-owned enterprises got paid, even if it was (maybe) a reduced proportion of their salary. Expat friends who were working at my school not only got paid, but also had a daily phone call from an English-speaking teacher at the school to check they were well, that they had taken their temperature and that there were no problems. I can't imagine that happening back in England where all too often foreign workers are seen as stealing jobs, not valued colleagues. Private companies had a harder time, as did the taxi drivers – but there are no real tales of hardship. (I guess I could try to find out more, but life is too busy and the questions I ask are sort of sidestepped.) All I can see is a country which had such a huge interruption in the routine of life but appears to have resumed normality very readily. In education, of course, it was helped that SARS coincided with the end of the school year (but a good two and a half months were lost) and then everyone returned in September for a new start.

So Beijing post-SARS is just a bit quieter, a bit less crowded – but other than that, normal. I seem to be the only person who even thinks it is odd that normality has returned so fast. But inside my head I keep wondering how come those three months of education, of exams, of tests, of progression into the next stage of schooling vanished from the system, with so little effect?

Apart from this huge question in my head, life here is – kind of – normal. I am living in a hotel, not my flat, but very close (the hotel I lived in for two months when I was first here, way back two years ago), so buses and shops and so on are all the same. But the landmarks have changed. Office blocks have been demolished; the skyline as I emerge from the underground has changed into a huge construction site (another shopping mall it seems). Actually I am using public transport less than before and I mainly use taxis. I am only here for such a short time, and am finding the jetlag quite hard to deal with, so there is no time in the morning to get up and catch a bus. It is a last minute dash, grab a cab and go. I have to have a map though, for the taxi to school – because work is being done to rebuild a bridge over the canal right by the school. If I asked for the school by name we would have to go right round all of this, adding a lot of time. So instead, I show the map, I then get out, dodge traffic and walk over the temporary bridge, and into the school. Easy when you know how – but to explain all this is way beyond my Chinese! (Mind you, the basic words have stayed with me, and I am happily surprised with the amount I can remember, and that I am still understood.)

After school I 'cheat' again, and take a taxi. Why do I think of it as cheating? Plenty of people use taxis as their means of transport – and it would be the same in London, or any other capital city. It's just I was so conditioned to using the bus and was proud of myself for becoming confident at using buses, at being able to manage. Taxis are a soft option, even if I do then have to handle the language, and risk the bad driving and decide if I'm going to wear a seatbelt – eccentric foreigner – or tough it out and cross my fingers as we hurtle, belt-less, across the city.

The seatbelt issue is stupid – we all know that. And yet, it is still a macho thing. The rules seem to be that passengers are okay without seatbelts, but the taxi drivers must wear them. So if we see traffic police, the driver (who is probably also talking on his mobile phone, but that will be tucked out of sight; hands-free has not yet reached Beijing) will then grab his belt and drive along, one-handed. With his other hand, which of course is his right hand, as this is a left-hand drive car, he will be holding the seatbelt as if it was buckled, but in fact he is just holding it there. And, when I reach for my belt (because of the law, because I do not like being driven by a one-handed driver), he will cluck and shake his head, to indicate that there is absolutely no need whatsoever for me to 'clunk click'; it is only drivers who have to do this.

While talking of traffic, I have just notched up another first for my time here. Earlier today I arranged to meet an examiner friend (expat) and his Chinese partner. Unlike so many of these couples, these two are much of an age. It is not the stereotypical ageing white male and much younger Chinese girl. Also they both are relatively fluent in the other's language. Her English is good (but that is not so unusual) and his Chinese is definitely fluent. Anyway, it was good to have a chance to see them again. We arranged to meet at a nearby hotel, which I walked to, but they arrived on bikes. We decided to go to another place, for coffee and a snack – but how to manage with bikes etc.? The solution? She jumped on his carrier, arms round his waist and I took her bike! This meant I had my knees knocking into my chin, and they were technically illegal, as pillion riding has now been banned, but it worked and we got there safely. At most junctions she jumped off, ran across (checking for traffic police) and then jumped back. But now I can say I have cycled in Beijing, on the roads, in the midst of the traffic. Once was enough. My decision two years ago not to get a bike was a wise one.

It was fun catching up though – and telling an IELTS examiner in China about the difference when examining in England. The beauty of IELTS (for students as well as examiners) is that it is an internationally standardised exam, the same the whole world over. It is internationally recognised by governments (for visa purposes), and higher education institutions (for study purposes), regardless of where you got it. And as an examiner I can earn money in China or in England. But the key difference is that in China you test a large number of students who all have the same native tongue. Back in England there are far fewer, but such variety. So examining in Manchester over the past month or so, I have tested Egyptian and Iraqi, Iranian and Austrian, Italian, Spanish, Nigerian and Filipino – as well as a fair number of Chinese. Odd, the transferable skills I find I possess. Who ever thought of earning a living as a travelling English language examiner? (Actually that is not a realistic possibility in England, but in China there are some who earn enough to live well, purely off weekend examining and some marking in the week. Well, until SARS came along and all the exams were suspended for a number of months.)

Anyway, I must stop. I am due out again soon – my evenings

are full, as I only have a short time here. I haven't really mentioned it, but the school is great. Lovely to see everyone again, to bring them news of the first group of students now studying in England (with some discreet editing, like the number who have found girl or boyfriends, alcohol and cars) – and to be teaching again. It is only a short intensive block of teaching, but I am also doing brief interviews with all of the Grade 3 students who may want to come to England. I see them alone, no teacher present, and just try to find out a bit about their motivation, their family situation (supportive? concerned? worried about money? definitely opposed but not wanting to say in front of Chinese teachers?). Of course, I cannot really know if I get the truth, but it is good to feel I am communicating, listening, maybe helping these young people. And it is impressive how much better their English is, compared with the equivalent group a year ago. SARS does not seem to have damaged their progress. For them it is also unusual to get this type of one-to-one tutorial, so maybe it is a good preparation for studying in England.

I must dash, but one more thing. It is so great to be here as an employee of the Chinese, with no link now to a university in England. It is humbling because they are paying so much to have me here, for such a short time. I feel I must fill every minute with work. But yet so flattering to my ego…

I'm off – for another heart-in-mouth taxi ride across the city, to visit Australian friends who live in a lovely modern apartment. Yes, those of you who had postcards from me in Greece this summer, these are the Australian friends who I last saw on an island in Greece this summer. Once you have the travel bug, you carry on travelling!

Love to all and see you soon – I am already halfway through my two weeks here.

Sue

2004

二
〇
〇
四

Dear Everyone,

Well, here I am, back again. And this time it doesn't feel so far away. More like a quick weekend trip. I am in fact here for ten days, but the sense of ease and proximity is due to my flight arrangements. Trying to juggle my new work arrangements in England with spending enough time in Beijing, I took advantage of the Easter bank holiday (Easter is not significant in China). But to do this I needed an airline with daily flights to and fro, not BA, which only has three flights per week. So using lateral thinking (and past experience from the time I flew back to the UK via Paris and Toulouse) I have flown with Air France, coming out on Easter Saturday Paris to Beijing, arriving early on Sunday, and I will return on Wednesday 21, ten days later. It gives me a recovery Sunday after the flight, seven full weekdays working at the school, and a free weekend in the middle to see friends and enjoy spring sunshine. But best of all I got a Saturday morning flight from East Midlands to Paris, so it really feels like a local flight. Home to the airport was thirty minutes (time to feed the cat before I left, have breakfast, and fret about anything I'd left behind), easy check-in. Lunch at Charles de Gaulle with no luggage as that had already been checked through; a bit of a stroll, and then on to Beijing. With a good book and some sleep it went fast.

Returning home I'll leave at a reasonable hour from Beijing (about 9 a.m., from memory); I'll land late afternoon local time in Paris, have time for a coffee and a bit of a leg stretch, and then a quick flight home to the East Midlands, landing at about 8 p.m. Yes, I know that is 3 a.m. on Thursday by Beijing time – but at least I'll only have a short drive home, can pick up fresh milk and bread on the way. Be in bed by 10 p.m. and work the next day, and Friday, and then a weekend to recover. It may not be quite as easy as I am pretending, but it does feel psychologically closer than doing the Heathrow run. And actually the cost is about the same – a cheap flight to Paris and then the standard Paris–Beijing fair. If this sounds manageable to you, then come with me next time I'm going to China! I can always find you some young Beijing students who will act as your tour guides in exchange for a chance to practise their English.

The other difference from other trips, and why I have energy to write this rather late at night, is that I have organised the teaching and the timetable rather than fitting in to the school's timetable. I suggested (and fortunately the school agreed, and it seems to be working well) that I will work with all the students who are intending to go to England in September. I will take all of them for the third and fourth periods every morning, 10.20 a.m. to 12.00 noon (two 45-minute lessons and a ten-minute break). Then I will take them in smaller groups, for mainly oral work, in the afternoon. They are all set written work every day, based on the lesson I have given them; they bring that in at 7.30 a.m. next day; I get to the school around 8/8.30 a.m., mark the written work, have meetings and then off to teach. This all may seem a bit boring and detailed, but believe me, after the flight and with the intensity of teaching we need to do, this is making a huge difference. Just removing the stress of having to wake up to be in for 8 a.m. to teach is fantastic. I don't have to be there to the minute because otherwise the class is unsupervised; this trip, if I am five minutes late, all I have to do is mark a bit faster.

I feel so much more relaxed and I also feel the students are getting a much more coherent course. It is quite intense, but they are responding well, and I feel we are building some real knowledge of business and business English, which should prepare them for the undergraduate studies in the autumn. For most of the classes I am joined by a Chinese and an expat teacher, so they know what we are doing and can reinforce it when I have returned to the UK.

I am also spending a bit of time with the younger students, in Grade 2, to tell them a bit about England. They are definitely less focussed and motivated – because it is still more than a year away? Or is it just that they have no interest in studying abroad? Who knows? Suffice to say they are considerably harder going in terms of behaviour than their older colleagues. There is talk of a parents' meeting, and I will also have a formal lunch with the soon-to-be-retired head teacher and his replacement. So the link with England should continue.

There is another bonus to all this: the school seems to have recognised that normal life can go on around me, so once the detail has been agreed I am left to get on with it. I have lunch with the staff, but then am able to go back to the office, or can sit in the sun. The weather is glorious. Beijing seems quite clean and clear, blue skies and warm temperatures (tee-shirt/short sleeve weather). So you can look forward to postcards, which I have written sitting in the sun at the edge of the playground. I laughed to myself as I was doing it; I could be an advert for VSO. The very obviously English, over-50s woman sitting writing cards home, as the children play basketball, or wander with friends, some stopping to chat to me and peer at the postcards.

But while I am at the school and it seems the same as ever, even down to sending postcards (and I'm in the same hotel, so using the same post office), so much has changed. It is obvious that use of email and the internet is gradually being embedded into the routine of school life. Which makes it much easier for me. For the first time I am not needing to spend time emailing from the hotel (even this I am typing on a laptop in my room, knowing I can save it to disc and then send it as an attachment on Monday. When I was here full-time I wrote letters from my flat, never from the school; even in October last year I had to use the hotel business centre). There are plenty of machines now at the school, all connected. Admittedly the Head of International Co-operation is not exactly IT-literate, so is happy for me to use his machine, but the previous Head of IC did not have a computer.

★

I stopped there, and got some sleep. So am now continuing on Sunday evening. I need some diversion before I go to bed – after today's hair-raising car experience – see below.

Talking about changes, and cars… another very obvious change is the playground – which is gradually becoming a car park. Not only does one of my expat friends drive to and fro every day, just as if she was at home in the West, but so do a number of the Chinese teachers. No longer does the head teacher's chauffeur-driven car sit in splendid isolation in the playground (for chauffeur, read 'driver'; slacks and a shirt, no uniform or peaked cap). Instead, there are four or five cars, of varying age, style, and mechanical reliability, parked in a line at the end of the basketball courts. There are still the bicycles, but I wonder how long before the cars will outnumber the bicycles. And it directly impacts on me – I still take a taxi to school, but get a lift back to my hotel, or to the shops, or wherever, with my colleague. Next week a visit to the Forbidden City is planned; I'll go in a colleague's car! I should add here that the visit to the Forbidden City is not arranged in my honour (although they all know how much I love it there and that I have visited quite often). No, the intention is to expose the students to some of their own Chinese culture before they go to England. As with locals everywhere, very few of these students have visited the tourist spots of their hometown.

But back to the cars. Beijing is now crowded with cars. Traffic does not move car by car, but more as a solid block of ten or fifteen cars which kind of creep forward like slow mud in a sluggish stream. The sheer weight of traffic is not helped by the incompetence and inexperience of the drivers. I am told that driving lessons are given on private sites on the edge of Beijing, where students are taught in pairs. One drives, with the instructor sitting beside them in the front; the other sits in the back, listening and watching – and learning? A genuine back-seat driver. And then they swap.

The test is both theory and practical – but only when you pass do you actually go on the road. Yes, all learning is done on the private driving school land, and then you venture out for the very first time, on the roads, for real, on your own – or with a very brave trusting friend! Another tale I hear is that when a new driver is in a crash, the police also ask where he or she was taught. And if an instructor gets a bad record, having a lot of ex-students in crashes, then the instructor's licence to teach will be taken away, as well as the drivers being sent back to school (with a different instructor).

And earlier today I had another hair-raising driving experience. I was in a rather flash car (owned by a private university on the north of Beijing, which I visited as it is looking for possible UK partners) – well, more of a stretch limo really. Smart driver (this one definitely a chauffeur), although the car was a little elderly. As with all such cars, there is a 'pedigree' attached – this allegedly belonged to someone in Deng Xiao Ping's government, and then was sold on and then sold on. Who knows? Anyway, we are returning to Beijing on the freeway (motorway) when it is clear that there has been a fairly major crash. The road ahead is blocked, traffic is being diverted off – but having been diverted off we are then allowed to go back onto the freeway. To do this, we drive the wrong way along a slip road (i.e. a slip road that traffic uses to get off the freeway, we use to return – feels very odd as the bends and arrows etc. are all pointing the other way). But it gets us back onto the carriageway, on our side, past the site of the crash so we pick up speed again to head towards the city. We are very honoured in being allowed to do this; most of the other traffic, which was diverted off, has to stay off. It is only because our car is clearly special, and no doubt has some special badge.

Anyway, there we are, hurtling towards Beijing, on an almost clear road when suddenly I see another car coming, at very high speed, towards us! Our chauffeur sees it too; for a moment as we swerve to the left the oncoming car also swerves, to its right; and then we swerve right and it swerves left (just as you do when avoiding a pedestrian coming towards you, and you end up colliding). We didn't collide – that's why I'm still here. But it was all very scary.

Who was the mad driver hurtling towards us, going at speed the wrong way along a motorway? The police. This is the way they get to the scene of a crash. The road is blocked, the traffic diverted off, so the carriageway 'downstream' of the crash should be clear. Apart from the great and the good, who, of course, are given special treatment. Thinking about it, maybe I realise why I feel like writing this letter rather than going to sleep.

One other, less stressful, mention of life and then I must get some sleep. Last night I went to dinner with one of my teacher friends. This has long been promised but somehow, in three years, we have not been able to sort this. But this time we have managed it. She arranges to come with her husband (she does not drive but they do own a car) and then we go to her flat. It is quite a way out – so I am yet again reminded of the distance she must cycle to work every day, in all kinds of weather. And when we get there I find another teacher is with her, who has helped with the cooking and making the dumplings.

The flat is tiny, but clean and obviously well loved. We enter the flat through a large hall, which would be really useful space, but has no natural light. It is a square room with a door off to the daughter's small bedroom, another to the small bathroom, another straight ahead into the kitchen, and one to the left to the parents' bedroom, which has a balcony. A round, folding trestle-style table is put up in the main bedroom, and variously using the bed, a small settee (for me, it's beside the bed), a stool and an ordinary chair, we sit round rolling dumplings. The bedroom also has several fish tanks in it – well, some in the bedroom and some on the balcony. This is her husband's hobby, breeding fish. It is calming, they explain. Calming maybe, but so little space.

Needless to say, the food is just amazing – *so* fresh, so tasty, and, as always, so much of it. In fact, some of it is prepared for freezing. We have made far too many dumplings, but a lot will be frozen for another day. The very large fridge is in the hallway. It is lovely being in a genuine home, but again I am reminded how lucky we are with the space we take for granted, the amenities we have, and how easy daily life is.

I must stop. I'll email this to those of you electronically connected; print off some copies and either post from here before I leave, or from England. More fun if I post from China though – all those exotic stamps. There is already talk that I will come back in the autumn to do some teaching with the next cohort. Too early for me to commit to this, as so much depends on what work I have in England. It would be good to come back, but I worry about the cost to the school. Can it really be worth it to them? Well, we'll see. Technically my contract runs until May 2005, so any of you who want to come with me, get planning. Fly out, (you meet your fare); I can swing you a free hotel room in exchange for you coming to do some teaching. And don't tell me you can't teach; English conversation is all that is required. So, if you're up for it, let me know.

See you all soon – just hope the weather in England in April will be as good as it is here – otherwise my Beijing acquired freckles will fade.

Love, Sue

www.ingramcontent.com/pod-product-compliance
Lightning Source LLC
Chambersburg PA
CBHW031128250726
48655CB00002B/565